ARCTIC
TO
ALPINE

Chuck Shipley
J.B.S. Publishing

Library and Archives Canada Cataloguing in Publication
Shipley, Chuck, 1939-
Arctic to alpine / Chuck Shipley.
ISBN 978-0-9733461-3-8
1. Shipley, Chuck, 1939-. 2. Game wardens—Alberta, Northern—
Anecdotes.
3. Outdoor life—Alberta, Northern—Anecdotes. I. Title.
GV191.52.S54A3 2008 363.28 C2008-903852-5

Cover photo: Canadian Rockies and Northern Lights
Back cover phoyos: Fuel Barrels on sled
                       Horse Patrol Ram River
                       Powder Magazine
                       Trappers Cabin Mackenzie River
                       Yours truly in the pictures
Cover Design: Francomedia.com
Editor: Carl Hahn
Copy Editor: Terry McIntyre
Reality Editor: Ron Leaf
Todd Dear Legal Advisor

Printed in Canada
First printing 2008

Disclaimer: (on advise of legal council)
The stories and incidents contained in this book are true.
The names of individuals involved have been changed or
omitted to protect their identities.
There is no intent to malign or denigrate anyone in the telling
of these stories.

Contents

DEDICATION iv
INTRODUCTION v
ABOUT THE AUTHOR viii
BRUCE'S MOOSE HUNT 1
CLEAN SWEEP 10
WATER, WATER EVERYWHERE 14
GOING NORTH 18
TOELESS AND FANCY FREE 25
TRUCK MOTORS & AIRCRAFT 34
FOX LAKE STORE 39
GRAVELY 43
BICYCLE BEAR HUNT 47
HIDDEN LAKE FISH 54
HELICOPTER SKULLDUGGERY 59
FLUSHER TRUCKS 69
DAM JUMPER 75
LOST HUNTER 80
TICK 88
TAR BABY 92
GRIZZLY BEARS AND TEA 96
DISSERTATIONS ON RELIEF 101
SEAMIER SIDE 107
DRAG RACE 113
BANG 118
MICHELE LAKES 123
MIDNIGHT TRAIL RIDE 129
RARING TO GO 147
BROKEN GRADER 151
FIRST BOW SHEEP 153
YELLOWKNIFE OR BUST 161
TRANSOM TRESPASSERS 176
EPILOGUE 182

DEDICATION

For her untiring inspiration and endless help I am dedicating this book to my wife Jean. The previous three books were only completed with her support and encouragement. Unselfishly she encouraged me to write more books even though she knew it would give her more work to do.

Our collaboration on; POACHER CHASER HOLIDAYS was a most interesting time resulting in a better book.

Thank You Jean

INTRODUCTION

Readers of my previous books, *POACHERS CRANBERRIES & SNOWSHOES*, *POACHERS BEANS& BIRCH BARK*, and *POACHER CHASER HOLIDAYS*, will find this one similar in structure: short stories written in a humorous vein.

As the title and cover information show, this book has a wide diversity of locations for its stories. From Inuvik in Canada's Arctic, and its round church, to horse-packing trips in the Canadian Rockies; drag racing 4-ton trucks in downtown Calgary. From there to New Orleans, where life is easy.

Stories of elk, bears, sheep, ravens, moose, fur, fish, turtle-hunting, broken equipment, Mountain pack trips, really bad behavior in a hotel, Mausoleums, fine food, plane rides big and small, oily kids, soaked cats, and many more.

Oh yes, and my favorite's about activities at -45 F.

ARCTIC

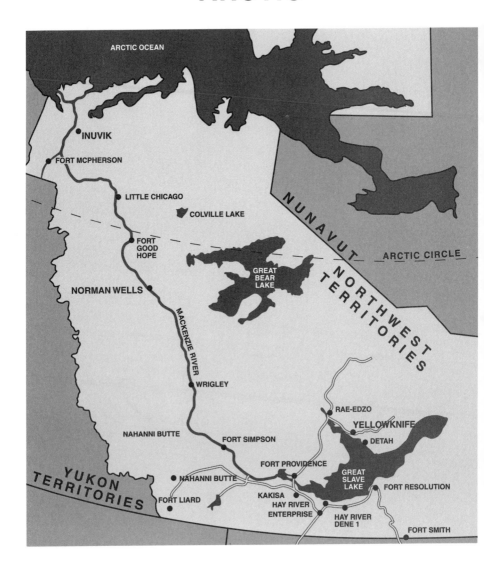

ARCTIC OCEAN

INUVIK

FORT MCPHERSON

LITTLE CHICAGO

COLVILLE LAKE

FORT GOOD HOPE

NORMAN WELLS

GREAT BEAR LAKE

NUNAVUT

ARCTIC CIRCLE

NORTHWEST TERRITORIES

MACKENZIE RIVER

WRIGLEY

RAE-EDZO

YELLOWKNIFE

NAHANNI BUTTE

FORT SIMPSON

DETAH

FORT PROVIDENCE

GREAT SLAVE LAKE

FORT RESOLUTION

YUKON TERRITORIES

NAHANNI BUTTE

KAKISA

FORT LIARD

HAY RIVER

ENTERPRISE

HAY RIVER DENE 1

FORT SMITH

NEW ORLEANS

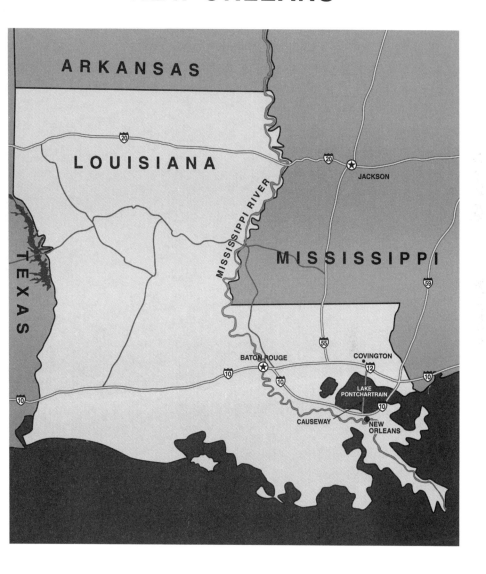

PACK TRIPS

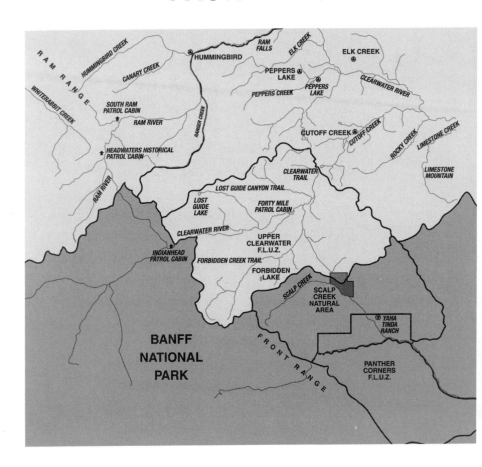

ABOUT THE AUTHOR

There have been two books about Chuck's career as a Game Warden;

POACHERS CRANBERRIES & SNOWSHOES

POACHERS BEANS & BIRCH BARK

The third book is a bit of a departure from these because it has holiday stories as well.

POACHER CHASER HOLIDAYS

This book containing the two types of stories, holidays and work has been very well received.

With its acclaimed reception and encouragement from its readers Chuck has written another;

ARCTIC TO ALPINE

This is a collection of stories as the title indicates is from the Arctic to the Alpine.

All written in the same johnera as the previous three books. Because it wouldn't fit on the cover it doesn't say anything about New Orleans or misguided escapades in Calgary. These stories are definitely one of a kind.

All factual and humorous

Chuck and Jean live south of Rocky Mountain House in their retirement home.

Apparently there will be more stories but he's not sure about what or when !!!

BRUCE'S MOOSE HUNT

Getting die-hard dairy farmers away from their second love is a chore of monumental proportion. My persistence exceeded the dairyman's dedication to his herd, and he finally agreed to accompany me on a moose hunt. The day finally arrived, and we were off to Carcajou, the location of Jean's and my summer and my hunting cabin. (The cabin is pictured on the cover of *POACHER CHASER HOLIDAYS.*)

Bruce and I were on our way early in the morning in order to get all the hunting time in we could. Five a.m. was almost too late for a farmer and a keen hunter.

The cabin was about an eight-hour drive away, so by leaving early in the morning, if all went well, we would have time to look around near the cabin before it got dark. A long drive with no excitement — just buying gas and having a roadside lunch.

As luck would have it, we arrived on the opposite side of the river from the cabin in the anticipated time. For those of you who do not know, our cabin used to be a Catholic Church. The Catholic Church ran out of parishioners and sold me their building and land. Subject of another story.

First the car-top boat had to be unloaded from its position tied to stock racks in the back of the truck. Next was the table.

The table at the cabin was no longer satisfactory, so we brought a campsite style picnic table — you know the ones with seat, legs and top all in one piece? It was not going to fit in the boat very well so Bruce suggested we float it down the river to the cabin. Carrying it from the truck to the river across the soft silt was awkward but we managed. The table was just buoyant enough that it would float upside down, so we started it downstream.

We quickly packed the remainder of our gear in the boat and started the 5-mile trip downstream to our cabin.

On the way we passed the table hugging the right bank, where the strongest current was. I was afraid it would run aground so we decided we would come back and get it. So far so good; we were about a third of the way there.

We arrived at the cabin without incident to find that, as usual, a bear had been to visit. The screen was ripped of the front door. Fresh bear claw marks showed on the inside wooden door. No denying who the culprit was.

Bruce and I hauled our stuff up to the cabin and finished up with enough daylight to go for a short boat ride and look for a moose. First we had to locate the table. Going upstream we barely got started and there it was. We got a rope on it and towed it to the Carcajou Store (pictured on back cover of POACHER CHASER HOLIDAYS landing, borrowed a truck and hauled it to the cabin.

All the usual migratory birds and their friends, filling the sky with their presence and our ears with their song, were at work! At this time of year along the Peace River in locations I am familiar with, the bird song is 24-7 for a good part of the fall. Our short evening moose hunt after delivering the table to the cabin was unsuccessful.

The next morning we were up early, noticing there was frost, which was not good. I am sure there are some things colder than riding in an open boat with no heat, but not many. A partial solution was at hand. I had an old canvas boat cover from a different boat that came close enough to fitting this one. We took it down to the boat and tried it on; sure enough it would work.

The idea was to tie the boat cover down at the bow, run its sidelines back to the oarlocks and through them to keep the cover from blowing away when we were under way. By bringing the lines inside, we could fasten them or hold them down with the gas tanks. One of the important modifications was the hole that needed to be cut in the boat cover, exactly over the second seat from the front. This was where Bruce would sit, his top half sticking out through the hole, the boat cover fitting tightly around his waist to keep the wind out. I was left to wrap what was left of the tarp around me, however I saw fit. Another triumph.

Lunch? Check! Guns? Check! Everything loaded and ready to go? Check. We're gone.

The frost had not started to melt when we left; however, our homemade cover kept us from getting cold until we'd traveled to a sand bar upstream, about an hour later.

"So what do you think?" I asked.

Bruce grinned, "So far this hunt is a real improvement. Remember the time we went home in the snowstorm because the steering cable broke on the boat? It snowed nearly all the way home. We wore everything we had and were still cold. The worst part, two days before it had been 90 above."

His expression all of a sudden changed as he continued, "I wonder what ever happened to the bear we saw that day with the bad front foot. It probably died."

I disagreed. "Bears have been killed and found to have broken bones that were healed. We saw the bear just after the steering cable broke is the way I remember it now."

We took another look up and down the river for either a cow or bull moose. Seeing neither, we got back in the boat to continue upstream. Secure under our tarp we traveled on, watching every break in the riverbanks, grove of trees, but mostly the shoreline.

The hunt brought us to the spring where our family went at least twice during holidays. We always boiled tea and had lunch while admiring the expanse of river.

This time we went ashore jumped around to warm up then tackled the river bank for an even better view.

The riverbanks on this turn in the river were grassy but very high, in the neighborhood of 200 feet. The banks always impressed me as on the verge of being too steep to have grass growing on them. Any disturbance dislodged some grass.

Bruce and I decided a hike up the bank would give us a better view up- and downstream as well as warm us up. Off we went.

It was not long and we were shedding clothes. Leaving our clothes to be picked up on the way down, we continued on. Warming up felt good. Nearing the top there was a break in the side of the riverbank with some poplar trees growing in it.

As we passed the edge of the poplar grove, what looked like bone could be seen sticking out from under some disturbed vegetation and sticks. A closer look with some rooting around revealed a moose skull.

"Look over here," I heard.

I looked but could not see much. As I approached, hair of the moose variety could be seen spread over a fairly large area.

"What do you think?" Bruce queried. "Looks like a moose kill but there don't seem to be many bones around."

4

"You're right," I replied, "it is a moose kill or it died of natural causes. Any way you cut it, the forest critters had a feast. Probably the bones got eaten or packed away. On that rib over there you can see the chew marks from something."

We dug around a little more, and then continued on to the top of the bank from which we enjoyed miles-long vistas of the river.

The binoculars came out and we started glassing, comfortable now that we were warmed by the sun and our hike up the bank. Our position on top of the bank at a bend in the river gave us an uncompromised view of great distance up- and downstream. We glassed and talked for about an hour. We both looked at things that could turn into a moose, but with both of us looking at them they never did.

"It has warmed up considerably; lets go upstream some more," I suggested.

Bruce was up and partway down the hill before I finished. We picked up clothes on the way.

It was warm enough the boat cover would not be necessary. We were around half a mile upstream when out of the bush, almost another half mile ahead, came a cow moose. We slowed the boat to the speed of the current and looked through the riflescopes at the moose.

"What do you think? She looks good to me," my partner said.

"It's your call. If you're happy let's see if we can figure out a way to get closer. Moose are not usually shy about boats till you get close but we cannot do that because we'd would have to shoot from the boat. I think the wind is from her to us so we can try and get a little closer, and then beach the boat. Hopefully we can find some stuff on the shore to hide behind while we sneak. She probably won't stay there long if she's by herself."

"Let's do it," was Bruce's only reply.

With that I got the boat as close to shore as I could without running aground and made some headway. While we were doing that, she went out into the river far enough I thought she was going to swim across. Our forward progress was stopped by a huge sand bar that would have forced us way out into the river where she would have seen us for sure. We decided to beach the boat and attempt a stalk along the riverbank.

With the boat tied to a piece of landlocked driftwood, we began our stalk. It was difficult, as the river flood plain is wide, flat and mostly silt or gravel. If we went far enough back to get in the bush, we thought she would be gone before we got close enough. She had finally stopped to drink, her belly in the water. I guessed she must have been tired of bending over to drink.

We got to within about 400 yards when she quit drinking and headed back for the riverbank. When she hit the shore she stopped.

"Do you think you can hit her from here? You may not get another chance," I said.

Bruce looked at me, then at the moose, then back at me. "The 06 has never let me down before," he said confidently. "I'll rest it on this log and shoot high."

Watching through my riflescope I could tell the bullet hit, she went down.

"Good shot! That's even better than your coyote shooting," I exclaimed.

I was standing up looking the other way when I heard, "She's getting up."

I spun around to look. Sure enough, she was headed for the bush. He took a quick shot but there was no reaction from the moose. She had now disappeared into the bush.

As I began to walk I said, "I'll take the boat to where you shot her; you can walk along the shore and see what kind of sign she left when she went into bush. It will take me a while to get back out into deep water and around the sand bars."

With that we were off. He reached where she went into the bush the same time I got to where she had gone out of the water. His arms were waving the "come over here" sign. After tying up the boat I was off. As I approached he said, "There's lots of blood — shouldn't be too hard to track."

Regardless of how easy she would be to track, the moose was heading away from the river. We did not want that. A hunter only has to pack meat a long distance once to learn that lesson.

Rather than press her, considering the sign she was leaving the river, we backed off for about half an hour. Every once in a while we thought we could hear her but were never sure.

"Let's go," I finally said.

We followed the trail as quietly as possible, it still showing lots of sign. Straight into the bush for a short distance, she then made a turn right back towards the river.

"This is looking better. Maybe we won't have to pack the meat that far after all," my partner said.

We stayed on the trail now, heading toward the river, wondering how an injured moose even with those long legs could navigate the windfall and flood debris we were climbing over. Finally we could see through the bush to the river.

"She can't be far now; there's the river," I said.

We struggled on, all of a sudden coming to a river backwater. There in the middle of it, head sticking out, was the moose.

"Well, it's close to the river but it looks like the water she's in is deep," was my partner's observation.

After surveying the situation, we concluded there was no way we could do anything without more rope to pull the moose to the edge of the backwater. That meant a run back to the cabin; more than an hour away. It was also getting late in the day — haste was required.

Traveling on the river after dark is fine, but we wanted to be loaded and on our way as soon as possible. A two-hour-and-something round trip with the boat would cut our daylight short.

As I pushed the boat off I said, "If the motor breaks and I don't come back, all you have to do is stay on this side of the river and start walking. You'll run right into the cabin."

He made some comment I did not hear as I was moving stuff in the boat. I got out into the river, turned, waved at him and headed downstream. I made better time going back; the boat was faster with less weight. In a little over two hours I came back around the bend, to see a fire in the distance on the sand bar where I had left him. Bruce had tea ready and I had the rope and more food.

"You weren't gone as long I thought you would be," Bruce commented as I neared. "I see you brought the rope but you didn't need to bring food; we have a whole moose to eat," he joked. We both laughed.

After tea and a snack we started working on the moose. We were able to get most of it out of the water. Our big concern was keeping the river sand and silt off the meat. To help with that, we had a tarp and plastic to put the moose meat on. After much toil and trouble, the moose was butchered into manageable sized pieces and loaded in the boat. We were both glad to sit down for the ride home on a dark moonless night. Our speed was cut by the 600 pounds of meat, bone and hide, but all was well.

As I remember it, we got to the cabin around midnight. To keep the ever-present bears from getting at the meat and destroying the boat we had to hang the meat. Confidence in our hunting prowess had prompted us to put a hanging pole between two trees, which is where we now hung our moose. That accomplished, we finally called it a day.

CLEAN SWEEP

During high school I had the dubious honor of working for the City of Calgary in various capacities. The highest paying job was a sweeping machine operator. After minimal training for a couple of days with an experienced operator, you were on your own on the job.

The sweeper of the day was called a Wayne. It had a metal bristled broom that cleaned out the gutters, sending its catch to a deflector, which lined it up with a large revolving broom that swept the refuse off the street and onto the conveyor belt, transporting it to a hopper to be emptied later. A sprinkler system to keep the dust down was always in action while sweeping, even though its efficiency was non-existent. Just for show.

An Achilles Heel to the whole machine was it's three wheels, with 4-ton truck tire size. Two were on the front where the hopper was and one on the back under the motor. No imagination is required to figure out a triangular shaped vehicle would take some getting used to, never mind built-in handling problems. The steering wheel was on the right, adding to the confusion. Get this: it steered by the single rear wheel. The only other triangular vehicles I have seen were of French design. Now there is a clue! You have the basic idea of what this machine looked like and its dynamics. Its height was approximately 8 to 9 feet. On with sweeper stories.

In Calgary there are underpasses that go under the railway tracks. The grade on entering or exiting is fairly steep. If you are a new operator on a three-wheeled, rather squirrelly sweeping machine, trying to get back to the shop on a Friday afternoon, you are in big trouble. Thankfully, the underpass was four lanes wide, because I entered it a little too fast. Initially everything was under control. When I tried to change lanes I was immediately propelled to the far side of the left lanes. Frantically turning the steering wheel that was on the wrong side of the machine, I narrowly missed hitting the centre cement abutments of the underpass. My frantic steering caused me to end up facing the abutment on the opposite side of the right lanes. More frantic steering, another close-up and personal view of the centre abutment. This went on two more times until the machine stared up the grade on the other side, where I was finally able to gain control. Oh yes, I was trying to use the brakes; however, they were totally inadequate for the job. With today's traffic there would have been an accident.

Spring cleanup is dirty and messy. All the sand and gravel that is put down over the winter to deal with slippery conditions ends up in the gutters to be picked up by the sweeping machines. Considering the inadequacy of the water being dispensed to deal with the wagon train-sized dust cloud I was making, things were going well. I used nearly all the water by the time I reached the end of the asphalt, turned around, and stopped at a fire hydrant to take on water. The hose from the sweeper's tank to the hydrant was strung out and hooked up. I was in the midst of opening the hydrant when a man pretty much out of control came around the back of the machine.

"What the hell do you think you are doing? I am going to have your job. Look what you did to my house you

#$%^&*^%##."

As he yelled and talked he was getting closer with each step and began to pose a threat. I felt fairly safe with the 2½-foot hydrant wrench in my hand that rose to a more defensive position with every step he took towards me. This, combined with all kinds of attitude that 19-year-olds have, caused him to stop. He said a few more words that are not printable and left. When I was sure he was gone I stepped back to view his house. It was directly across the road from me: a nice-looking, ordinary house, the kind with four boards of siding at the bottom then stucco to the roof. One thing did not look quite right. The siding on the back of the house was a very attractive chocolate brown. The side next to the road I just swept was the same color as the road. No wonder he was mad.

I finished filling the water tank, raised the brooms, went a block and started sweeping again. Three blocks later the foreman showed up. Surprise, surprise! He pulled up in his little green truck. I climbed out of the machine. He was not smiling, not even a little. A jovial "Hi!" did not help. I knew I had done nothing wrong; apparently he did not think so.

"So tell me what happened," he said.

"Sure."

The only thing he questioned me on was if the man had told me the house was freshly painted.

I said, "No way! I'll bet you could get fired for covering a new paint job with road dust if you had been told it had just been painted."

He finally smiled. "This is not the first time this has happened, nor will it be the last. See you at the shop at 4:30. The city will pay to repaint."

"Now why would they do that when he did not tell me he

had just painted it?"

"It's called public relations," the foreman said, got in his truck and drove away.

That was the last I ever heard about that.

In Calgary there is an event called the Calgary Stampede. Sweeping machines are required at intervals during that parade, especially after the horses (of which there are many) to sweep up the horse droppings. On one occasion I was asked to operate a sweeping machine in this prestigious events parade. I was only too pleased to comply. A whole day's pay for two hours work. How could I turn that down?

The day arrived. I was lined up in the parade staging area, ready to go. Horses in front, Majorettes behind. Cleaning up for the ladies seemed an admirable duty. We started off at 2 to 3 miles per hour. If you know me or have read any of my other books you have to know slow speed is a fate worse than death. The only compensating feature was the 2-hour view in the sweeper's rear-view mirror.

On that day two other things were interesting. A lot of parade observers would yell, "You missed some horse pucky!" You had not. Even if you had there was nothing you could do about it.

Next time you go to a parade where there are sweeping machines watch and listen to how many watchers cheer and clap for the sweepers. There are lots

.

WATER, WATER EVERYWHERE

Ice is interesting and somewhat like people. At first glance you do not know if you can trust it or not. Experience teaches that ice is hard and inflexible when you fall on it. This may be because we lack mass — well, some of us anyway. Ice's ability to withstand impact or pressure is directly related to its quality (lack of trapped air in the ice) and thickness.

In my previous books, the construction of ice bridges gives some idea of ice use and how strength is related to thickness. The elasticity of ice is a whole different matter. Vehicle speeds are kept down on long stretches of ice bridges or ice roads to minimize the wave effect of the water beneath the ice, so when the water wave under the ice contacts the shore the ice is not fractured.

A story in this book about an ice bridge on the Mackenzie River might give you the idea that folks on the crew would have considerable knowledge about ice and its quarks and quirks. Not all the time.

We were traveling towards the Mackenzie River on freshly prepared cutlines, the cats barely staying ahead. I do not know who made the decision that we had to camp for the night or where. Usually the cats cleared a place at the side of the cutline to set up camp for the night when we were on the move. That did not happen this time. A cat trail was made onto a small lake whose surface was partially cleared.

14

All vehicles were parked close enough to the power plant to plug in, affording light and fan use so the guys on the top bunks would not melt from the heat generated by the oil heating stoves in each trailer. Usually the trucks and trailers were unhooked when we camped; fortunately not this night.

My memory is a little fuzzy on the exact events that night. I think we had supper and returned to our trailers to settle in for and evening of reading.

Suddenly the door opened. "Get the trucks and trailers off the lake! It's flooding!"

A message like that guarantees results, particularly when it's -40 F and everything could be frozen in, in minutes. Flooding on a lake you are parked on could be catastrophic.

Peering out the door while putting on my jacket, I could see the water rising very quickly through the snow that was left on the ice. Looking around some more between the trailers I saw the problem. There was a column of water about 3 feet tall and 5 inches wide shooting up through a hole in the ice. My first thought was that hole was man-made; this is not Yellowstone.

"Quit gawking around and get out of the way! We have to move!" This statement, coupled with a shove and a glare from one of the old hands, got me going.

I leapt out the door into 2 or 3 inches of slush, which was the result of the water mixed with the snow left by the cats when they cleaned the ice, I was heading for a truck cab. Halfway there, everything went black and nearly silent. The power plant had been shut off.

"Unplug the trailers and roll up the cords!" came the party chief's voice through the darkness. I headed for the plug-in on of the other side of the bunk trailer. One of the guys was already there. Our eyes were getting used to the darkness. A glance down showed the water had risen another couple of inches. My feet would soon be in danger of getting wet. This could cause instant frozen toes. I was not going to let that happen. We rolled up the power cord and threw it on the truck attached to the generator.

The water was still rising. I made my way back to the truck as carefully as possible so as not to get water in my boots. The only thing that kept my feet dry as the water rose was the coverall legs over my boots. It was so cold that when the water splashed as you walked it froze on your coveralls instantly, making the lower pant leg stiff and keeping it tight up against the boots so the water could not get in

I jumped in the passenger side just as the driver started the truck. Now there was a lineup to get off the ice that was proceeding way too slow for anyone's liking.

If too much water flowed out from under the ice to hold it up, the ice would star cracking away from the shore. We would have no chance of making our escape from a cold, dark, watery, icy grave. A look back showed the plume of water coming out of the ice had not diminished in any way, even though some trucks and trailers were off the ice. We were still way too far from getting off the lake as far as I was concerned.

The truck headlights finally lit up the trees on the shore and we were the second truck back from getting off the ice with our bunk trailer. One last look back. With over half the equipment off the ice, the water column started to diminish. It looked like we would be OK.

After we were all on the cutline, strung out like a wagon train, the party chief came along with more good news: there would be no power. "Get out your flashlights; it's going to be a long night."

Well, at least we had heat, which is very important when it's -40 F and some folks are wet. However, not much later, and without the benefits of the fans, those of us on the top bunks were complaining about the heat as those near the floor froze.

Some organizing went on during the night, which was lucky for us. The organizing got the cook trailer in position to hook up to the generator to allow the cook to make breakfast and lunch for the coming day's journey.

Over breakfast we found out about the water problem. The camp attendant was told the camp water supply was way down. Wait your getting ahead of me!!!! Anyway, his common sense and ambition were not working at full capacity, so he made a hole in the ice just outside the cook trailer door so he could pump water directly into the water tank. He was the brunt of considerable ridicule for some time.

Water, water everywhere.

GOING NORTH

What an experience. Just 18 years old and off to a job other than delivering prescriptions for my Dad or working for the City of Calgary or farming. The City of Calgary was my employer during high school and one summer after.

The first seismic experience was rather short-lived. We started at the company yard in Calgary driving trucks to a place called Keg River, 120 miles north of Peace River town on the then-new Mackenzie Highway #35. Checking the map, it looked (and was) a long way from Calgary, and all of it north.

I was assigned a three-quarter-ton loaded with who knows what. Picking up a fellow at the Lacombe trailer court was my first assignment. He would take over driving since he had been with the company previously. Things started to go bad just south of Bowden on Highway 2 north. A red flashing light appeared in my rearview mirror. Yes that's when they were only red and single. I pulled over to the shoulder. The officer advised me I had a taillight burned out and wanted to know where I was going. I told him. He said I would have to get it fixed at the nearest garage before going further. A warning ticket was issued and I drove to the garage at Bowden that was in sight of where he stopped me. Hmm, I wonder?

I pulled into the garage to see the closed sign being put up. I stopped the truck feet from the door jumped out and ran to the door. He heard me and turned to see what was happening. I blurted out, "The police just stopped me and said I had a burned-out taillight and had to have it fixed before going any farther. I sure hope you can help me; I am traveling with a seismic crew to Keg River."

"That's a long way to go north with a burned-out taillight. I think they just got a new highway up there. My neighbor has a friend who traps up there somewhere; he came back talking about how great the highway was. I will open the door. Bring it in and I'll fix it."

"Thanks! I really appreciate that, considering you were closing."

"On these long, dark, November nights there is not much to do, so might as well work. Don't have TV yet."

Thanking him again for this trouble and stuffing the receipt for labor and the bulb in my pocket, I was off for Lacombe. When I arrived one of the other trucks was there waiting at the trailer where the new driver was. We all exchanged a few words and my driving was over. Off again to a motel in Peace River for the night. Finally, we were all together again ready for the last leg of our journey to Keg River.

I had not been this far north before, so was very interested in the view from the truck. Who knew there was all this farming going on so far north? Then it had only been going on for 30 to 40 years. Leaving Peace River we had to cross the Peace River on the train bridge. I do not need to tell you that trains had the right-of-way, size-wise and ownership-wise.

As I drove across the train trestle, I was amazed at the width of the river. Being from southern Alberta and only having seen the Bow and Elbow rivers, this was impressive. I read about the paddle-wheelers and steam-powered boats on the Peace.

Now I understood.

Now there is the same old train bridge and a two-lane vehicle bridge. Both bridges have huge cement pilings. The side facing into the current is shaped like a boat prow, very sharp to deflect ice, logs and debris. At another time I saw the pilings in action. The current carrying 100-foot trees and ice at floodwater speed impacted the sharp pilings. Trees snapped and ice crumbled, driven by the surging power of the floodwater. We crossed the bridge without incident. Up the hill on the other side, we turned at last where there was a sign that said Keg River.

We got to Dixonville about 40 miles north of Peace River when one of the 1-ton trucks pulling a bunk trailer put a connecting rod through the oil pan. This meant it needed major repairs. No time for that. The trailer had to be unhooked and put on another truck. A location was found to unhook the trailer and leave the truck. Jacking up on the trailer tongue took the trailer weight off the truck, so it could be pulled away and another truck hooked up to the trailer. Simple plan?

This is where it all went south. A Jackall jack was located, put under the trailer tongue and jacked up to where it took the weight of the trailer off the truck. There was a spring-loaded trailer hitch on the truck. The spring mechanism on the hitch had to be held open, allowing the hitch ring on the trailer tongue to pass through it. I had that job. I signaled the trucks to go ahead. I was looking at the drivers who had their heads out the window watching for my signals. There was a slight metal-on-metal scraping noise. I looked and saw the Jackall falling from under the trailer tongue towards the back of the truck. I yanked my right foot back — not quite quickly enough. It was partially pinned under the trailer hitch as I yanked, it did not hurt. My toes did not seem to want to work right. Others had seen what

20

happened and were sure my foot was broken. Off to the Berwyn Hospital. The fellow who took me there in a company half-ton said, "You shouldn't take your boot off till you get to the hospital, then let them do it."

I was not listening and he shut up. I had on rubber overshoes with wool slippers inside them and wool socks. Nice and warm. I eased all that off. There was not much blood or pain. When the sock was finally off, I could see the big toe had a half-turn to the left, and the next toe was pulled off where it fits onto your foot, so you could see the whole joint. I took them all in my hand and gently squeezed. The whole thing felt like hamburger. I looked at the driver; best I can remember he was a pale shade of green.

It did not seem very far to the Berwyn Hospital. I have vague recollections of the driver saying he was going as fast as he could on the icy roads. By the time we arrived at the hospital I had put the sock, slipper and overshoe back on. I thought I was going to walk into the hospital. I turned as I opened the door and put my feet out. All of a sudden there was immense pain and dizziness. I was glad the driver had hustled around to help me into the hospital.

Without all the details, the big toe and second toe were amputated in Berwyn. I asked to have them put in a bottle of alcohol so I could keep them. The answer was no. I protested that they were mine and I should be allowed to keep them. No response. You need something to show your grandkids that other grandparents do not have. That was my chance. I wanted a chance to have a toe in a bottle like the one in the Jack London Story of the Klondike Gold Rush.

After a week in Berwyn I flew to Calgary and went home. My first night at home, complete with cast from foot to knee, I started throwing up in the middle of the night. I had to go on hands and knees to the toilet to throw up — too weak to walk. Dad called the ambulance and of I went to the General Hospital. With in hours I was in the operating room having the cast removed. Some time later the doctor came in.

"How are you doing?"

"At least it does not hurt any more. When can I go home?"

"You had the last laugh this morning. When we took the cast off the smell nearly knocked out all the operating room staff. You had a severe case of gangrene. To make your foot as good as possible we have to clear up the gangrene then check for what else needs to be done," said the doctor.

"How long will all this take?"

"That is very hard to tell. A lot will have to do with clearing up the infection. Your doctor in Berwyn did not contact me about the medication you were on; that is why the gangrene got started. You can rest up here and get hydrated. After that we will see what can be done."

I got put into a ward with nine other guys on the fifth or sixth floor of the General Hospital in Calgary. I was pretty dopy from the drugs and anesthetic but before long I could get around in a wheelchair. Biggest mistake they ever made.

A guy I went to high school with was brought in the next day with a broken foot. We talked about old times (as many as there are when you are 18!) while the cast on his foot hardened. The next day he was allowed to use his wheelchair. Trouble. We toured the hospital from cafeteria to roof.

Next morning my doctor showed up.

"I want to have another look at your foot to see how it is progressing." He looks; I do not like what he says after. "We need to give you a general anesthetic so I can do more work." He tells me he booked the operating room for tomorrow morning. "The faster we get this done, the sooner you will be able to go home."

"I am with you there, I'll be here."

It turned out there were seven operations on my foot, including the one in Berwyn. Oh yes, and a skin graft. Skin was taken from my stomach area to replace the skin I pulled of yanking my foot from under the trailer hitch. The graft extends from the base of the toes up the foot about 2 inches. Even for an 18-year-old full of piss and vinegar, that many operations with a general anesthetic within an eight-week span made a trip out the windows from the sixth floor look attractive. A passing thought.

Between the operations there was mischief to get up to. My old schoolmate and I had wheelchair races in parts of the hospital that were not too busy, but not for long. One of our biggest coups was barricading ourselves in the TV room. Sending 18-year-olds to bed at 10 p.m. was not acceptable, as far as we were concerned. We got quite a talking-to about that, but guess what? There was a head nurse who understood and let us stay in the TV room till midnight as long as we were quiet and keep the volume turned down. Staff's tail really got in a knot on this one. We started to race to get on the elevators.

After pushing the button to call the elevator, we would back our wheelchairs to within 5 or 6 feet of the elevator doors to let passengers off, if there were any. We waited there gripping the wheelchair wheels as far down the front as possible, looking over our shoulders, watching the floor numbers change. Tension mounted as the doors started to open. No passengers! A Herculean heave back on the wheels and we were careening backwards towards the elevator door side by side. Almost there. One more heave would do it. Something went wrong. I was starting to see ceiling tiles. Ceiling tiles turned into the elevator door jamb. I was in the wheelchair on my back, looking up at the ceiling in the elevator.

"Are you all right?" asked my racing partner.

"Yeah. Help me up before the nurses get here."

"Too late; we're here." I looked up between my knees. Oh crap, it was the crabby one, with help.

"What do you think you are doing? I'll bet you were racing to see who could get on the elevator first."

We must have looked guilty. Her next statement was a winner.

"You could get hurt you know!"

We started to laugh hysterically, tears coming to our eyes. Telling two teenagers in a hospital already in wheelchairs they could get hurt was over the top. The nurses did not see the humor in it. My wheelchair was righted; I sat down and we were both told that behavior would not be tolerated. We disappeared down one of the halls to plot other mischief.

Some good was done while we were there. Hospital procedures were not as rigged as they are now. If any of the nursing staff needed anything taken to another nursing station anywhere in the hospital and were in a hurry to get it there, guess whom they called on. This went fine till some top-level admin folks noticed an increase in efficiency in certain areas and made some inquiries. That's when the wheelchair express ended.

An oversight. If you are ghoulish and or detail-oriented you will want to know this. The right foot has three toes amputated where the toes emerge from the foot: the big one and the next two. The other two were badly broken but healed OK.

The Mounties said that's why they wouldn't hire me.

Hospitals are what you make of them. Time to go home and recover. That took a while and is another story.

TOELESS AND FANCY FREE

Well you have read about the squished toes; now, if you are curious, the recovery may be of interest you.

With the operation over, hospital mischief at an end, it was time for me to go home. I had broken up with my girlfriend during my stay in the hospital so I was looking forward to dating upon my release. On my first day out of the hospital, I'd arranged a date, with one of my friends driving the car. (We all know there is no time to waste on matters as important as dating, particularly when you are 18.)

With the cast covering my foot and running halfway up the calf of my right leg, you might see why I couldn't you drive myself. At that time I had a vehicle with a standard transmission; lifting the foot and leg with the partial cast would not work well.

It was not long and the cast came off — as I recall, less than a month. The next problem I faced was that the leg muscles had atrophied monumentally, almost down to nothing. Physiotherapy at the Belcher Hospital in Calgary was the next step. Now that the cast was gone I could drive myself to the hospital. For those who do not know, this hospital was a facility mainly for war veterans. I won't describe the injuries I observed other than to say losing three toes was a minor inconvenience in comparison.

The first day at the Belcher was interesting. A doctor, with no introduction or fanfare, sat down opposite me. "Good morning. Let's have a look at your foot."

I lifted my foot for him to see. It was as atrophied as the calf muscles and was white as snow. It did not look that good.

Turning it sideways, up and down and every other direction you can think of, his final conclusion was, "It has healed up nicely. The skin graft has taken well, but you will never be able to walk properly or do the things you used you do. The physical therapy will be of some help. Good luck." And with that he was up and gone.

My first thought was, "What does he know? It does not hurt and I can walk on it. We'll see about that."

Physical therapy started immediately. A nurse was assigned to work with me three times a week. Basically the treatments consisted of massaging the skin graft on top of the foot, and me making the small and next toe (the only ones left) work — moving them up and down or clenching them towards the ball of my foot.

I'll let you know, having a nurse massage your foot, particularly when you are 18, will cause blood to drain from your feet, so you're not able to perform well in that area.

The treatments lasted for two months. By the time they ended, I was able to flex the toes and pick wooden matches off a tile floor with out a problem. The therapy, in conjunction with total leg exercises, soon had my right leg as good as the left. The only remaining problem I faced was sharp quick turns to my left. I learned quickly that one's big toe on the right foot is important for balance and stability, particularly when turning to the left.

At the end of the treatments, my mom and dad decided to

go to New Orleans to visit my mom's sister. I was invited to go along.

My uncle was the vice-chairman of a prominent American insurance company whose head office was in New Orleans. I knew he was going to be way too much fun when Dad and I went at his invitation to have a look at the office building. He was about to start the building tour with us when he got a call.

"Excuse me I will be right back," he said and then asked the secretary to take us on the building tour. She pointed out all the interesting things we could see in a seven-storey office building, even the executive bedroom, bathroom, and kitchen that "Uncle" had attached to his office. This appeared to be rather extravagant but interesting. Just as we finished looking at his office, he reappeared.

He looked at the secretary saying, "Thanks for doing the tour; it is hard to get away from those guys in Bogotá." He then turned to us, looking at my dad, and said, "So what did you think of the building and the tour?"

Dad, being his honest self, spoke of a number of interesting things we had seen in flattering detail. "I am glad you enjoyed the tour and were impressed with the building; actually it's just a seven-storey house of ill repute."

Dad looked a little shocked but laughed with the secretary and me. I was beginning to think that this trip might be OK after all.

Anyone who has visited New Orleans knows you must go to the French Quarter. At that time it was the entertainment center of New Orleans. All kinds of shows, magic, jugglers, dancers and strippers were there, all of which were most uncommon in Calgary at that time.

Uncle was running the tour of supper and clubs; we all

followed. In front of all the entertainment establishments was a barker extolling the virtues of the entertainment inside.

Before I go any farther, you need to know Uncle's job, besides being the company VP, was entertainment coordinator for head office. When the company reps came from every country in the South and Central America and all over the U.S., he was the man who knew where the action was.

We passed a number of barkers on the sidewalk selling their employer's wares. I remember wondering why none of these places were suitable. Uncle looked at my mother and said, pointing, "This should be OK for Calgarians." We trooped in; Uncle looked after the doorman.

A show was in progress with four scantily clad ladies doing a dance number on a little stage. Their scanty attire becoming scantier by the minute. They stopped short of naked, just. This was all pretty heady stuff for Albertans, back in the late 50s when a stripper was someone who used paint stripper.

Anyway, drinks were ordered and we all sat around talking and watching the show. It was not long till the show ended and the ladies left the stage to sit at the bar. That's when I heard Uncle say "Chuck". I looked at him; he was beckoning me to come over to his chair. I got up and went around the table, bending over when I got to him so I could hear what he was going to say.

"Here's $20 — go sit with the dancers." He was looking at me with a most mischievous grin. "Come on, you won't get another chance like this."

My blood was doing the same tricks now as when I was getting my feet massaged by the nurse. Now the $20 bill was in my face.

"Last chance. They won't stay there all night."

Right then I knew I had the coolest uncle in the world. Unfortunately, or possibly fortunately, I declined because my mother was three seats away.

Uncle also had a summer place across Lake Pontchartrain, just out of New Orleans. There was a 25-mile long causeway across the lake, which is something we'd never seen. It had a couple of built-in hills to relieve the dead straight boredom of the drive. We saw barges on long lines being towed under it. I wondered if the barge captains ever hit the bridge pilings with the barges.

Over the causeway, a short drive through a little town of Covington, and we arrived at Uncle's house. What an interesting place: 10 acres covered with pine trees, and a modest house with banana trees at the front door. A short distance away was a two-bedroom, fully equipped guest house. On further looking around, Uncle revealed a creek with a white sand bottom.

"See the turtles?" Uncle asked.

"Boy there sure are a lot. How come they are so nervous?" I asked.

"Everywhere but here they are shot at or somehow captured and eaten. I think that makes them nervous."

"No kidding."

"Would you like to shoot some? The boys up the road shoot them, take them home and eat them — mostly in soup."

"Sure. What kind of gun do you have?" I asked.

"I don't have a gun, but we will go to town and buy whatever kind you want."

What kind of response could I give but "When do we leave?"

A 2-mile drive to town found us in the hardware store. I kid you not; it was just like the stores you see in the very old Western movies, all sorts of stuff hanging all over the place. My focus was quickly drawn to the glass gun case with a selection of pistols like in a gun catalogue. Rifles of all calibers and makes lined feet of the walls.

"Pick whatever one you want," said Uncle. Again the coolest uncle possible.

We ended up with a Harrington Richardson .22 caliber, double action, nine-shot revolver and lots of shells.

Back to the house and down to the creek went Dad, Uncle and me. After about the sixth shot Aunty and my mother showed up, apparently drawn by the shooting. To say Aunty was hot under the collar over the pistol would be an understatement. There were words between her and Uncle.

I kept using the pistol till we left some days later. Who knows what happened after that? I still think he was one cool uncle, but I am quite sure that after we left there was no more turtle shooting going on.

My aunt had a son who was older than me, but was away with the navy. She tried to compare my eating to his. Why? Well during my stay in the hospital I lost 30 pounds, going from 170 to 140. In the three weeks we were in New Orleans I gained back 25 pounds. I ate pretty much anything that couldn't get away, and loved every morsel.

We had the opportunity to dine at some posh restaurants. Menu items included food you were expected to eat with your fingers: fried chicken, ribs, seafood and the like. By now you know that, in my world, if humor can be generated it is my obligation to do so.

Here's the setting: a posh dining establishment, white linen tablecloths, linen serviettes in rings, more cutlery than a Sears Catalogue, customers and staff dressed to the nines. A scrumptious meal, ending with flambéed strawberries (Yeah, they burnt them!) was duly consumed. During this magnificent feast, a small clear glass bowl appeared with a lemon slice floating in water in it. Uncle and I are the only ones who got these. I had never been to a restaurant where I received one of these before. I was watching him to see what to do. He did nothing with it and we were almost ready to leave, I felt obliged to do something. I was taught it is not polite to leave food or drink.

"Maybe it's a drink," I thought. "It's in a glass bowl."

With that I picked it up with both hands and brought it towards my mouth. I had my lips all ready to accept the edge of the glass when, "Charles! Don't!" rang out at about 200 decibels.

I stopped, looked at Auntie and then looked around. People at the near tables were looking. Sitting upright, bowl in hand, I did not move. To my right I heard an unfamiliar noise. I looked; it was Uncle. What I could see of his face, which was partially covered by his serviette, was beet red all the way back into his receding hairline. He unsuccessfully tried to stifle his laughter and appreciation for the situation at hand.

"You're supposed to wash your fingers in that and wipe them on your serviette," Aunty stated, glaring at me and pointing at the bowl still held at my pursed lips.

Keeping eye contact with her I brought the bowl even closer to my mouth. Her mouth went agape, eyes widening. At the last possible moment I slowly put the bowl back on the table.

Make no mistake; I had no idea what the lemon water was for when it arrived. But on its arrival I started looking around. Sure enough there was someone dipping his fingers in it at another table, and individuals wiping their hands on a serviette.

You have discovered reading my books an opportunity lost never returns.

Later back at Uncle and Auntie's, Uncle sought me out. "The old girl hasn't been that excited since Ed left home. You didn't know this: after we sat down some of her society friends came in. She was terrified you were going to drink the lemon water and that they would see you. Good job!"

"If she had been quiet probably no one would have noticed anyway." I replied, "I wasn't going to drink it until I found out what it was for. I was only looking to see what someone might say."

By now Uncle is red again. He turns to leave saying, "I can't wait to tell your aunt that; she figures no one can trick her."

I could hear him laughing as he went down the hall.

One of Auntie's society friends owned a cemetery, handed down through the family for generations.

"A cemetery tour," declared Aunty, "one like you have never seen before."

"This had better be different," I mused to myself. "I can see cemeteries at home."

The cemetery tour day arrived and we were at the somewhat ostentatious front gate. We were announced and entered. On the drive to the office we saw a mausoleum for the soldiers that died in the American Civil War. Ceremonial cannon balls were stacked in front. A mausoleum in this case is a structure built to house the dead. Mausoleums had been used in this area prior to the civil war, as the water level was so high nothing would stay buried.

Arriving at the cemetery office, we were greeted by the owner, who started the official tour. You've probably guessed there are all types of mausoleums, presumptuous and plain. Some were built with marble imported from Italy, some with marble from Georgia. As far as I can remember, there were no wooden ones; they were all some kind of rock. We went into a number of them. Inside they were like filing cabinet storage rooms. Names and dates of the occupants indicated their space.

The Civil War mausoleum was the most interesting one, mainly because it was one of the oldest. Each drawer showed name, rank and serial number. There is one wrinkle left to tell in this story.

Over time, due to human interference, the water table dropped, allowing conventional burial with modifications. The plot was generally raised a foot or two above the normal ground level. Now the internment could be accomplished without an above-ground structure. However, the increase in dry ground attracted some unwanted guests: fire ants. While the little critters did no harm to the interned, they were bad for business. Perception is what it's all about.

Overall the tour was different, but not spectacular. It was also our last outing before we came home.

TRUCK MOTORS & AIRCRAFT

Christmas is coming, time to leave the Arctic Circle and go home for Christmas. About four days before Christmas, a single engine Otter arrived at our camp. It would take us to Inuvik on the Mackenzie River and a flight to Edmonton and Calgary. We were ready when the plane arrived, after being in the bush for about two months. One of our crew stayed to make sure our camp did not freeze up while we were gone. I was under the impression he was handsomely compensated.

The flight was uneventful over the Tundra to Inuvik. Upon our arrival we were taken to the hotel to wait for the chartered DC-4 that would take us non-stop to Edmonton. It had been chartered by Heiland, Century and Western Geophysical to take their staff out for Christmas.

As the various crews arrived, they were brought to the hotel as we had been, to await the arrival of the Pacific Western Airlines plane (Please Wait Awhile) DC-4. Biggest passenger plane of the day. Most of the crews adjourned to the bar, as the camps did not allow liquor. As we were one of the first crews to arrive, it was still light enough to have a look around. Rather than go to the bar, some of us took a walk around. The Utiladors were a new thing for me. This is a square or rectangular box mounted 3 to 4 feet of the ground on H shaped stands that takes guess-what to all the building in the community. Utilities, sewer, water and heating, and whatever. Electricity used the conventional poles. There was also a round church, supposedly so the Devil could not corner you. Really, it was done in that fashion to resemble an igloo. To ensure that, it was white. The large residential school was close at hand as well. A Canadian Navy base was also there, but it did not look like a navy base.

When we finished or tour and went to the bar I soon found out a number of the folks on the other crews were acquainted with some of our crew. We had been there a while when a couple of the party chiefs showed up.

"If you guys want a flight home there is a planeload of cargo that has to be unloaded before we can go south."

Our party chief chimes in, "Anyone who does not help stays here for Christmas."

I was pretty sure that would not happen, but I wanted to see how the plane was going to be unloaded so I jumped on the bus with the others. When we got to the airstrip there sat the DC-4. It looked to me like the cargo doors were 10 to 12 feet off the ground. You need to know this was Inuvik, 1958. There was no airport equipment at hand to unload the plane except a small portable ramp that could be extended from the ground to the cargo door. That was fine for the small stuff that would fit. Some of the cargo would not fit properly on the ramp, so it was balanced best as possible and sent groundward. Some stayed on the ramp and some did not. Amazingly, none of the items that bit the ice at the bottom appeared to break. This all worked fine. The cargo was loaded on trucks after it got to the ground and hauled someplace.

Now the interesting part. A six-cylinder motor appeared at the cargo door. It would not fit on the ramp. In fact, I do not remember anyone even trying it. I wondered how the volunteer unloading crew would deal with the motor. It was not a long wait.

Just inside the cargo door where people on the ground could not see was a winch mounted with an extending arm to give clearance, so when you attached something you had room to swing it clear of the fuselage and lower it to the ground. To the best of my knowledge there were no air crew or airport staff on hand to assist with the unloading. That is bad enough, but to charge seismic crews, probably close to 60 people in number, some of whom had been drinking for a time and wanted to get home NOW, any way to unload the plane was acceptable.

All eyes were on the cargo door opening, watching as the hand winch cable was put around the motor and hooked to itself. A half-ton truck was backed up and parked beneath the cargo door to receive the motor. With some effort, the two men unloading the motor cranked the winch up enough to get the motor clear of the aircraft's floor. They swung it out into mid-air with considerable enthusiasm. So much enthusiasm the motor swung like a pendulum. Before they could lower it or stop the swing, it came back and hit the side of the fuselage. They let more cable out than the length of the extended arm, allowing the motor to swing back more than the length of the arm and hit the fuselage with enough force to severely bend the aluminum — maybe enough so we could not fly.

You may guess at the language and threats being used by ground observers as to the intelligence of the unloading crew and vice versa. The motor was swung back into the plane. A few cranks on the winch shortened the cable. A piece of plank was seen in one of the unloader's hands.

With unwavering attention we watched. Out the door swung the motor. It arched back, desperately trying to hit the fuselage so we could spend Christmas in Inuvik. Try as it might, it could not outwit the man with the plank, who placed it right were the motor had previously hit and hit again. Somewhat chagrined at not disabling the plane, the motor dangled at the end of the cable. The arm was pushed out horizontal to the plane, the motor lined up over the truck. The unloaders were attempting to release the stop on the hand winch so the motor could be lowered in to the waiting truck. Success was not forthcoming. Patience was wearing thin. Heckling started. That did it. A man with a hatchet appeared. One mighty stroke with the hatchet and the taut cable was severed. The motor was on its way to the truck box, air express from about 12 feet.

When it hit, the front wheels of the half-ton, short-box, 1950-something Chevy came off the ground. A huge cheer came from the crowd. We all ran to see the damage to the motor and truck. The motor looked fine but the truck box, factory-made with 6-inch planks and metal support strips, did not do so well. Two of the planks were broken, and the surrounding metal bent. The motor had gone through the box. A decision was made by someone that the motor had to be unloaded. Who knows why? How to do that? I tell you, the ingenuity never quit. We had tow ropes. There were a series of 2-foot, barber-painted posts along a taxiway.

"Back the truck up to one of those posts," said the party chief.

It was backed up, a tow rope tied around the motor, the other end to a post, with lots of slack.

"Back up some more; you need to be touching the post." That was done.

More direction from the party chief. "OK. Rev the motor as high as it will go and drop the clutch. We'll pop that motor out of there."

Sounded like maybe he had done this before. After two tries it worked. The motor did two complete turns in the air and finally landed on the frozen ground on its oil pan. Again we all went for a look. Visible damage was to the oil breather pipe. Who knows what we could not see? Anyway, that's where the motor spent Christmas. Incidentally, it was not ours, so I do not know if it ever ran or not.

In case you are interested, we flew out shortly after. I don't know if anyone told PWA about bending their plane with the motor.

As we approached Edmonton, the word went around that heavy fog may cause us to go to an alternate airport like Calgary. That was fine with me. The Edmonton folks were not happy. We could not see outside very well as it was dark, but it appeared there was fog. Within minutes of this information the plane bounced once, twice and we had landed. So much for the heavy fog.

It turned out our pilot had a reputation for finding holes in the fog.

I doubt you can have this kind of experience any more!

FOX LAKE STORE

During the summer months the Fox Lake Hudson Bay Store was only accessible by boat or plane. There were two places to make winter roads: one east of Fort Vermillion, the other east on highway 58 till you got north of Fox Lake. There you turned south down a seismic line, went across an ice bridge on the Peace River, and then you were there.

My trips to the Fox Lake Store mostly took place one of the two ways mentioned. A drive from Fort Vermilion was a little long due to road conditions: crooked narrow and rough. Smooth sections were nearly non-existent. One was the crossing of the Wabaska River. On the back cover of *POACHER CHASER HOLIDAYS*, there is a picture of a raft built by trappers resting in the spring run of water of the Wabaska. These rafts were fairly common on larger rivers, built to haul trappers, fur, dogs and anything else the trappers brought out from their trap lines. They were used once to reach a destination and left to float away on high water. A full description of raft construction is in the above-mentioned book.

The next river crossing, the Little Red had a grass airstrip just upstream of the winter river crossing that was used by private pilots from High Level. They fish there annually when the walleye run is on. From here it is still a bit of a drive to our destination. Fox Lake had one main street. It passed the HBC

Store and Fur Warehouse continuing on to a hall at the end of the street. The hall is used for many occasions; one is annual payment of treaty money to the local Indian band.

Going into the store we found the manager and asked him where the fellow lived who the policeman was looking for. The only housing was some log cabins and small cookie-cutter Indian Affairs houses. Directions to a residence were interesting. No street signs — you turn at this house, go to ... you get the idea. Eventually we located our suspect. He was interviewed notes taken and that was that for now.

On our initial visit to the HBC store we were invited to stay for supper if we had time. Of course we accepted. It did not matter whether you drove home in the dark or light; you drove at 40 miles an hour. We were in the police van (Chevy panel truck, single red, bubble-gum-machine light on the roof) of the day and that was its speed on a winter road.

I checked the fur books. It listed the date, trapper's name, address, trap line number, and a column for each type of animal with a box to put the number of pelts from that particular animal in. Pelts in the store were counted and matched to names in the book. To finish the job we went to the fur warehouse.

In my experience this was one of the few H.B.C. stores that still had a complete fur warehouse. It was a building about 12 by 16 feet square. Upon entering you were met by the fur press dominating the buildings interior. It was obviously a device to press things — in this case animal pelts. The pelts were pressed into bales of 90 lbs till about 1866; then the weight was lowered to 80 lbs. It was still used in the late 60s, when the pelts were pressed and shipped by truck or aircraft to their final destination.

With the counting done and all pelts accounted for according to the book, we went to the house for dinner. At that time the

HBC store fronted on the street with the fur warehouse to the side and back a bit. Joining the store, fur warehouse and house was a raised wooden sidewalk. With the house set back some distance from the store it was obvious by the snow piled on each side of the walk it took some effort to keep its considerable length clean.

We enjoyed a wonderful supper of meat, potatoes and vegetables with Saskatoon preserve pie. Each plate arriving emitted copious amounts of steam into the room, an unequivocal contradiction to the inch-thick ice on the inside of the windows inches away. Did I forget to mention it was another -40 F day?

On a tour inside the house we saw personal memorabilia from other previous HBC postings across the north. The only similarity to other HBC houses was the furniture. Must have been bulk buying going on.

After a chat and tea it was time to head into the night. Donning our coats and thanking the host we were off. Opening the door, fog immediately formed thick enough that my partner ran into me coming out the door. This was met with gales of laughter from our hosts. Somehow this prompted a race down the wooden sidewalk past the store to the truck, which was never turned off but locked while running.

Some distance down the sidewalk I heard my partner yelling something. I suspected a ploy to get me stopped so he could pass me and win the race. My speed increased. I heard him again. More speed. We're getting close. BANG. A pistol shot!! I knew he wasn't shooting at me. Nobody could miss from that close even with a pistol.

I glanced over my shoulder just in time to see the muzzle flash and hear the bang from a second shot. We're at the truck now.

"What the Hell was that all about?"

Holstering his pistol he said, "After we had such a good time running down the sidewalk, it seemed like the right thing to do." I agreed as we got into a very warm police van. Out of Fox Lake we entered the seemingly endless black and white tunnel whose length and width were what the headlights made it.

Some hours later in Fort Vermilion I unplugged my truck. The interior heaters, block heaters and house insulation stuffed everywhere I could fit it made it warm enough to jump in and drive away, home to High Level.

What can I say, another interesting day?

GRAVELY

You have no idea how lucky you are when you get work-related instructions first thing in the morning and then are sent off for the day to do your job. For part of one summer I had a job like that in the company of a strange little machine.

After minimal instruction I was assigned a half-ton truck with this strange machine in the back called a Gravely. The Gravely is like a low-end garden tractor. It has handlebars, to steer; instead of a rotor to dig it has a 4-foot cylindrical brush rotating counter-clockwise to move loose gravel. So you do not have to walk behind it there is a seat on wheels attached by way of a trailer hitch ball to the Gravely. That of course means when you are backing up, unless you are careful, the seat will turn the opposite direction to the Gravely. This can upset the whole outfit or just stop movement depending on how fast you are backing up.

The sole purpose for this machine is to sweep the loose gravel off the pavement where oiled streets meet pavement. If this is not done the gravel will eventually work its way onto the pavement. Traffic leaving an intersection where there is gravel on the pavement my spin its wheels, inhibiting merging into traffic, or shoot the loose gravel back into the intersection hitting other vehicles and pedestrians.

At 8 a.m. assignments are handed out. I had my list of streets and avenues for the day, somewhere in southwest Calgary near the long-forgotten drive-in theater. Leaving the Manchester City yard it took a few minutes to get to my destination. Upon arrival I parked the truck and backed the Gravely out of the truck box on two planks spaced so the Gravely tires would go down them. Adjusting the lever to start, I set the choke, pulled the starter rope and was in business. I always unloaded before I started the Gravely, because the trailer seat tended not to follow the planks and I felt sure, given the opportunity, it would have pitched me of.

I started at one end of the assigned street at the first gravel intersection and worked my way down one side, back up the other side to the truck. This particular street runs north and south so I was sweeping either east or west. With a gale-force west wind I started on the east side of the street so the wind would be at my back.

Nearly half finished on that side a very peculiar thing happened. One the northeast side of the corner a woman appeared at the back corner of a house, her mouth agape. (I assumed she was yelling at me, but I could not hear her for the noise of the machine.) She began waving her arms frantically as she ran toward me. Always the optimist, I thought she may need some type of assistance. I thought, "I work for the City; I am here to help!"

I drove the machine over to the curb in front of her house and stopped, turning it off. By then she was in my face yelling, "You can't do that! You are getting dust on my house!" While she was yelling her arms and hands were flailing about indicating wind direction, dust patterns and the lack of sense I had to be doing what I was doing. She finally finished her rant, at which time I suggested she did not need to yell. She gave me a look that could kill, but I was only 18 and had lots of lives left — not to mention that I was assigned to clean up the corners on this street.

"I will not stand for this! You are making a mess."

We were standing on the gravel in the intersection, the west wind blowing around 25 to 35 miles an hour. It kicked up dust all around us and none was blowing anywhere near her house. It was going towards the house across the intersection from her. She finally had to stop for a breath. Now was my chance.

"Ma'am, as you can see while we have been standing here the dust has been swirling around us and all of it has blown towards your neighbor's house across the street from you. I have been assigned to clean all the intersections on this street and I intend to do that."

With that I turned and got back on my machine and went to work. In later life, diplomacy would guide you to go to another intersection. Not a chance. I was right and I knew I was right.

She disappeared around the back of her house. Thank goodness I had made a couple more passes with the sweeper. She reappeared. What was she doing? A water hose in her hand?

I kept sweeping and she kept coming to the front corner of the lawn closest to me. By now I was about as far from her yard as I could get while sweeping. What was she doing? She's got to be kidding. She had the hose on and was trying to soak me. Water was arcing towards me. Oh darn, didn't make it. Not enough pressure, hose to short.

Two more passes and I was done. She finally quit when I was on the last pass. I looked back as I went to the next intersection to see her gathering up her hose and shaking her fist at me.

She phoned. The foreman and I talked. Move to another intersection even if you know you're right if that happens again. I grudgingly agreed.

BICYCLE BEAR HUNT

Bear hunting on your mountain bike seemed to be a good idea. We had a spot picked out where lots of bears had been seen. Bike across the foot bridge on the North Saskatchewan River and go west to the old sawmill site instead of Siffelur Falls. There were a few creek crossings along the way just to get our attention. We waded the creeks while pushing the bikes.

I do not think bike riding is permitted there now. On the new maps it is called Glacier Trail. It used to be an old logging road that ran from the south end of where Lake Abraham ends to the Banff Park border and beyond. If you look closely you can see the old bridge pilings the loggers put in upstream from Preacher's Point at the south end of Lake Abraham.

We started out at the Siffleur Trail parking lot down the trail to the suspension bridge on the North Saskatchewan, across it over to the old logging road going west. Here on the Kootenay Plains, in the early 1900s, was a horse ranch. A micro-climate stretching a short distance up and down the river maintained a more moderate temperature than the surrounding area, ensuring less rain and snow but lots of food for the horses.

My partner wanted to know where the horse trap was. He apparently remembered one of our previous conversations about the amount of horse traps around the Nordegg area, and this one in particular. We stopped at our first creek crossing,

Louden Creek, the only one we didn't have to wade because someone put a plank across it.

"It's just back there and up the hill. Do you want to have a look? We could leave our bikes here and walk up there," I said, pointing south up the hill.

"No" he replied. "It will take too much time from our bear hunting."

With that we were off, crossing more creeks, sometimes riding across, sometimes pushing our bikes. Finally we reached the edge of the sawmill site and stopped for a look around. No bears to be seen.

"Lets have lunch; I'm starved," I suggested, and we started looking for a place to eat and watch the old sawmill site for bear activity.

"Good idea. How about over here where we can see most of the site."

We pushed our bikes to the chosen spot, unloaded our lunch and sat with our backs up against some handy trees.

"So tell me about the horse traps. I did not know there were so many."

I replied, "I know where there are a few, I am told there are lots more. Down highway 940 just up the hill on the south side of the North Saskatchewan on the west side there's one. South of the Cutoff Creek there's one and there's some around Nordegg. The old-timers will tell you there everywhere.

"Coming in where I pointed one out to you, that's an interesting one. It uses a creek canyon and dead trees to help guide the horses. Interestingly, the canyon and all the ground on both sides is covered with grass and sedges the whole length of the trap. There are no trees and hardly any bush. You do not want them in the way when you are trying to herd wild horses to someplace they may not want to go.

"When you walk up the hill the first thing you see is a line of gray old tree trunks stretching along what turns out to be a creek canyon. Getting closer to the creek canyon itself, you see the tree trunks are set in a V. You have come on to the V about halfway down one of the arms. The arms go past you to your right and left. They continue on to a bend in the creek you cannot see around from where you are. An estimate on the each arms length is about a mile.

"Apparently the idea is to round up some horses and get them headed in the direction of the open end of the V. Then you put pressure on them to gallop so they do not notice the dead trees are hemming them in. By the time they realize that, they are at the apex of the V. There is a corral there with a person hidden to operate the gate, closing it after the horses are in the corral trapping them. There the horses can be sorted and fed if necessary. A small natural spring is in the corral the horses use for water.

"Some of the other traps are different. A corral is built where you know there are wild horses. Late in the spring when the horses are not as healthy as they should be from meager winter feed, quality horse food is put in the corral. When the horses are passing by they can smell the food. The smell attracts them to the corral and they go in. They will activate a trigger device when they begin to feed. It closes the gate. You do not have to be there all the time; you just check the trap and pick up the horses. That is a short rubdown on what I know about horse traps."

"That's interesting. How long has that one we passed been there?"

"I don't know for sure but I was told the wings used to be two or three trees tall. If you go look at it now the trees are all flattened out and really decayed. Maybe since the horse ranch; who knows? It's so dry here it takes a long time for stuff to decay," I replied.

"Enough talking and eating; let's go look for a bear. How about we follow this trail along the creek that parallels the east side of the sawmill site and see where it goes? We can leave our bikes here."

I was not hunting, just there for the fun of it. My partner picked up his rifle and we were off down the trail. Visibility was good in all directions, about 100 to 200 yards. We were not talking and making very little noise on the green growth under foot. The wind was in our face.

"Did you hear that?"

"No," I answered. "What was it?"

"Sounded like some kind of grunt. Let's go over behind that bush," he said. "We'll be able to see better from there."

With that he was off, with me right behind him looking in the direction he indicated the noise came from. We both got behind the bush and crouched down. The bush was about 6 feet tall and 3 or 4 feet wide. Standing part way up, we could see through the bush.

What do you know, around 75 yards away there were two medium-sized bears sniffing, digging and fooling around. There was a short discussion about size. A decision was made on which one was biggest. My partner wanted a better shooting position, so he got down on his knees and crawled into the bush we were behind. It was so thick I could not see him even though he was only a couple of feet away.

The bears were still digging, rooting and sniffing. Best of all they were getting closer. In fact I was wondering when he was going to shoot. One stood up to scratch its back on a tree. That was the time. Stone cold dead at the foot of the tree. The remaining bear woofed and ran off into the bush.

Now the work started: skinning and looking after the meat. By the time the bear was skinned the hunter decided the only meat required was a little from the hams. That was just fine with me. Packing jiggly stuff on a bike, even when it is secured in a bag, is interesting on crooked trails and creek crossings. Loaded, we were headed for the truck.

At one of the creek crossings we stopped for a drink.

"One of the guys in town said there are more trails out here on this side of the river. We've only been on this one. Where are the others?"

"Just past this mill and to the south there are a number of interconnecting trails that used to be logging roads going up the side of the mountain. That's where we can go next time." I answered.

"Have you been up there?"

"Yeah, quite a few times. It is one of my favorite places to go with the mountain bike. You can get to Banff Park. I went as far as I could but there was a bunch of deadfall across the trail so I stopped. On the trails that go up the mountain I have always seen quiet a bit of bear sign, mostly grizzly. Nice big tracks in the mud along the trails.

"You can't tell how steep the grade is up there till you get there. When you are going up you are using all the little sprockets on your mountain bike. Coming down is fun and could be faster but for the condition of the trails and some nasty turns limit that.

"On one of my trips up there I was on the last big downhill stretch to the main trail. There is a nasty turn in that downhill stretch about halfway down. Visibility is limited because the bush along both the sides is drooping over the trail in some places and high in the rest so you cannot see around corners. I had come far enough through the corner I was able to see a little way ahead. There was a bear right on the trail.

"I grabbed the brakes and started hollering my head off, not knowing which way to turn. The trail's too narrow to get off of. The hollering was not doing much good so far. Surely these guys cannot survive if they are deaf. Finally a look, but no action. The distance was closing fast, way too fast for me. I tried to turn a little sideways to make the back wheel skid sideways. Had to be careful because there was rock sticking out of the road. Could tip you over. Wouldn't the bear feeding right in the middle of the trail love that: fresh lunch. Meals on wheels so to speak!

"The bear was finally paying attention now. After the look and a second's hesitation, it was off down the trail in front of me, going as hard as it could. I was still catching it. Who knows how bears act if you try to pass them with a pedal bike? I could not get off the trail for the bush.

"One look back, a higher gear in the bear gear box, but still going down the trail. I was right on his bum. Finally it dove into the bush and was gone, leaving nothing but waving brush 12 feet high. I continued yelling looking sideways to see if I could see anything. Just swaying bush. That gets your attention.

"That's a story about the other trails. You know, there was one thing that bothered me about that bear. As I rode back to the truck I thought it must have been watching too many movies or TV shows," I said.

"Why would you think that? It was a bear; you're losing it," my partner said with a fitting look of concern for my mental state.

52

"Just a minute. You watch TV and movies. When someone, bad guy or good guy, is being chased with a vehicle, they never immediately go to one side or the other to escape impending peril; they run straight ahead just like the bear did. Explain that?"

"We know the movie guys script what goes on. That takes care of that. I don't know; the bear must have thought it could outrun you. In spite of your weird bear, I want to go up there sometime. Sounds interesting, but we better go or we won't be to the truck by dark."

We made it back to the truck before dark. The bear meat was excellent. I cannot remember if he got the hide made into a rug or not. It was a grand day, as are most.

HIDDEN LAKE FISH

Everyone thinks game wardens know where all the best fishing places are. That is not necessarily true. They think they know where they should be. Most of the time the ardent fisherman whose life's passion is to find the best fishing spots knows the best spots. You should know there are some game wardens that do not either hunt or fish. Even without the intimate knowledge derived from partaking of these activities, which would help a game warden when tracking the elusive poacher, they do remarkably well at their profession.

On one occasion it was my privilege to accompany two local fishermen, Wayne and Bud, to a lake in the mountains west of Nordegg that later became a hot spot for trout fishing. Fingerlings were stocked a number of years prior to our trip there, but the lake was hidden well enough hardly any one bothered to check on the fish growth or just forgot.

One of the stories going around was the lake was so well hidden the only people who knew where it was were the government staff who stocked it. That being as it may, the government fish-stocking list came out, and one of my sharp-eyed friends spotted it had been stocked again. This jogged his memory, reminding him some years before it had also been stocked.

The phone rang. "What do you know about Hidden Lake?" was the first thing I heard.

"Never heard of it," was my response.

"Well that's good. Apparently a lot of other people have either forgotten or have not read the fish planting lists because I just found out there are lots of catchable-sized fish in there from a Red Deer fellow. He says you can't keep them of the hook."

"Who was it?"

A long pause. "I can't remember right now but he's one of the guys from Trout Unlimited. Always keeps up on all the best fishing spots."

"Do you know where it is?" I asked

"Not exactly. He said it is just down the trail from Land Slide Lake towards the Kline River and there is no trail to it or indication on the Landslide Lake Trail where to go east. How about you asking for better directions and we can take a trip in there?"

The "we" referred to the three of us. I went on many memorable trips with them, skiing, hiking, fishing and hunting.

"You bet I will. I'll call you back as soon as I find out some thing."

"Okay," was his response and we hung up.

The next day I made inquiries about the lake and its location. I was told it was about a mile northwest down the Landslide Lake Trail, off the east side of the trail not more than 700 yards. I was also told there was no noticeable trail because it was stocked by helicopter, and tree cover in the area was very dense. The next evening I phoned to answer the questions.

"I found out a better location than you had and it has catchable-sized fish, but they aren't very big due to their numbers — and growth is slow in mountain lakes anyway."

"Well I made a call for more information to the fellow who was there. The best he could do for directions was talk about a tree with a weird bend in it so far up the Landslide Lake Trail from where it branches of the Lake of the Falls Trail on the west side. Some help but not much."

"It's better than what we had before, Anyway after looking at the map it does not look like there is much room between the trail and the mountain on the east to hide a lake of any size. What do you think?" I asked.

"Let's go look. It's a horse and hiking trail to where there is no trail to the lake. We'll ride our mountain bikes as far as we can and then walk."

Phone calls were made. The three of us were geared up to go the following Sunday, as one of the guys had to work Saturday. Arriving at the Kline River staging area, we unloaded our mountain bikes, loaded up our packs and fishing gear and were off down the trial. It was a bit of a grunt pedaling in, but with 21 gears you could pedal most of the hills, though loose rocks were a problem. Looking forward to the fast ride out helped.

We arrived at the junction of the Landslide Trail and the Lake of the Falls Trail. We knew we were getting close. We started looking for the tree with the weird bend in it. Apparently it was not weird enough because we missed it. The next thing we saw was the north end of Landslide Lake.

"We've come too far; there is Landslide Lake," Bud said.

We all took a look and decided, given the limited distances we were working with between the trail and mountain on the east, we would spread out in a line from the trail to the east at 50- to 75-yard intervals and walk north. I drew the straw that put me farthest to the east, which was on the slope of the small mountain that was east of the lake. After we got lined up we started north, almost immediately finding the tree cover very dense in all directions.

After a few minutes of fighting through the bush I heard,

"Do you see anything?"

"Can't see for the trees. Its pretty steep up here, should be able to see something soon."

More trudging trying to see through trees.

"I see it. It looks like it is straight down from me. You guys must be right there. If you keep going you will hit it."

I started down to the lake. By the time I got there, they were both standing at the south end of the lake.

"Not much sign of fishermen here," said Wayne.

We agreed and started walking along the west side of the lake to see if we could find any human activity. Sure enough two-thirds of the way down the west side there were signs of a tent or two and shore grass packed down on the shore from anglers standing casting.

We stopped for a look into the water. Wayne pointed and said.

"Look! There are three fish — not very big but big enough to eat, pan size."

"Well the trail should be just over there" said Bud, pointing to the west and starting to walk.

"Let's go stash our bikes, get our stuff come back and catch fish."

We followed him out to the trail, stashed the bikes from I am not sure who or what and headed back to the lake. Stashing is always good. Gives you peace of mind, till you cannot remember where you stashed whatever.

Back at the lake we geared up and started casting. Flies, bait or small spoons hitting the water were immediately consumed. There was no stopping them. After three each we quit, made a fire and started frying fish. They just fit in the small frying pan we brought.

It was hard to get your fill so one of us would fish and the others would cook and eat. There are few tastier ways to eat fish than fresh out of a cold mountain lake cleaned, into a frying pan cooked over an open fire with salt, butter, lightly browned.

I have to pause now to get a cloth to wipe of saliva. I can still taste them.

We stayed there for a couple of hours after our fill of fish, just catching them and putting them back.

"Time to go don't you think?" I said.

In unison: "Just a few more casts."

We all started casting again. About an hour later a consensus was reached on leaving.

Back to the trail, we loaded our bikes and were off down the trail. It was a hairy ride, Wayne in front, me then Bud. We slid around corners, powered up small hills, jumped roots, and went as fast as we could without falling, barely in control. We were looking good, almost to the truck. I thought I had enough room to look back and see where Bud was. I turned my head and there he was coming as hard as he could about 20 yards back. I turned back again and somehow a 6-inch pine tree had miraculously grown up in the middle of the trail. I tried to miss it but clipped it with the left handle bar. I was out of control heading for the ground, all the while thinking how close Bud was and that there would not be room for him to stop or go around me.

The next thing I knew he was stopped by my legs that were still out on the trail. He ran over the lower part of the right one and I did not even feel it — well not till the next day. Wayne had looked back, seen the pile in the trail and come back to investigate. We were all surprised I did not have a broken leg, but it worked fine. Bad bruises the next day. Anyway we got to the truck and home, with stories to tell.

HELICOPTER SKULLDUGGERY

This is a story about some of the skills I have seen helicopter pilots use while performing their duties. One of the first ones was at Barrhead when we were thinning the wolf population in the Swan Hills by poisoning. (That's the subject of another story.) At that time (early 60s) helicopter time was at a premium, but somehow my boss got time for us to fly over the Swan Hills to check for the best places to set wolf baits. I should tell you that was the one and only time we saw the helicopter. After that it was by Skidoo (now called sleds).

We hired a professional trapper to assist us. Our flight commenced from Barrhead, then on to the trapper's farm near Neerlandia to pick up the trapper. Having had little experience with helicopters at that time, I could not wait to see how it all worked. Taking off is like going up in an elevator mounted on the outside of a building, with the side of the elevator facing out all glass. You ascend smoothly with objects on the ground magically becoming smaller by the moment.

Arriving at the trapper's farm we landed on the road in front of his house. Before we go any farther, you need to know this was before burying all the wires in and around your farmyard was done. We were hovering just over the road when the pilot turned the helicopter to line up with the driveway, like you would a truck. He then proceeded to fly up the driveway inches off the ground under a number of high voltage electrical wires to the house. The trapper came out, ducked down, approached the open helicopter door and got in. As he was getting his seatbelt buckled, the helicopter began to back up. For a first-timer in a helicopter, this was astounding to say the least. To add to my astonishment, he continued to back down the driveway to the road. I cannot be sure of the distance he backed up, but it was between 30 and 50 yards. Later I was able to ask the pilot about the backing up exercise.

"I would not normally back up that far, but I misjudged the room in the farmyard to turn the machine around when we flew over, and there were too many wires to take off but there was room to back up," he responded.

"Thanks. This is my first time in a helicopter. I don't think a lot of people know they will back up."

"You're probably right, but it is handy. Glad you enjoyed the ride; I have to get back to Edmonton."

With that we shook hands and he left.

Seeing pictures and news coverage of helicopters lifting drums of fuel, tranquilized bears and other cargo is commonplace. With these items it is easy to know the weight you are expecting to lift. Herein lies the problem: neither the pilot, my partner nor I were able to estimate the weight of the two dead horses that had been reported to us. Fish and Wildlife does not usually have anything to do with horses except to ride them, unless their demise affects wildlife. Their welfare is the responsibility of another department.

A slight aside from the helicopters. It was early spring west of Rocky Mountain House when there used to be a grizzly bear season. These two horses died in prime bear habitat on a trapline whose owner reported their demise to us. Was it an accident or had they been taken to the site and killed for bear bait? Not uncommon. The upcoming bear season was why we were concerned about dead horses. Dead horses are not uncommon, as there are numbers of wild ones, but this location and time were suspicious.

The horses had been dead for some time, so they were frozen through and through. The trapper, upon discovery, looked for signs of cause of death but found none. Other than being dead, they appeared to be in good shape!

These were big horses — not as big as a Clydesdale or Percheron, about halfway between that and a saddle horse. The trapper had guessed 1,200 lbs each. That's what we had to go on. Another problem was they were frozen to the ground, showing at least they had arrived at the location alive.

"So what do you think? Can you lift one of these the way they are?"

"I don't know. If the weight guess is close, once we get it loose from the ground I should be able to," the pilot said.

"Can you try to lift the horse now, so we can see where we have to cut it loose from the ground?" my partner said.

"Sure. Hook the cable around the neck behind the head and we will give it a try."

That was done, a strain put on the cable and the head and part of the front quarters came out of the snow. One of us went under the hovering helicopter with an axe as the pilot continued to apply tension to the cable. Lucky for us, there was lots of snow that year, so we only had to deal with cutting frozen snow to get the horse loose. With the help of the helicopter we had the horse free from the ground in minutes.

Prior to this exercise getting underway, the pilot had been advised we wanted the horses put in our trucks that were about a mile away. The reason for this was to have them necropsied in Edmonton as to cause of death.

When the pilot saw us both clear of the horse, he pointed towards the trucks. We gave him the thumbs up. The power went to max, and the horse we thought was the smallest began to leave the ground. Power increased. The horse gained altitude, but not much. The pilot tried for more forward momentum. Apparently things were not going right because the next thing we saw was the horse dropping from 20 to 30 feet in the air, ending up almost where it started. I had always wanted to see something dropped from a cable on a helicopter and now it had happened.

The helicopter landed and the pilot shut it down. While walking over to us he said, "It's not much too heavy, but I have to get over those trees to get to the trucks and it was going to be to close. (Horse people do not read the next part.) I can fly back and get a chainsaw so we can cut them in half; that will be an easy lift."

"That will take a while," I said. "If we take turns with the axe we can chop them in half in about the same time it will take you to get a chainsaw, and we won't be standing around here shivering or building a fire."

If you are interested in receiving a look of sheer astonishment, try suggesting this to someone. Anyway, the helicopter stayed; we took turns with the axe and got the job done. The horse parts ended up in Edmonton. The results of examination were they had been shot at close range with a small-caliber firearm. We did not find those responsible.

The working relationship between helicopter pilots and field staff is very high. There is a prime fishing lake southwest of Rocky on the North Fork road called Gap Lake. Ice fishing is very popular because you do not have to fight the muskeg to get to the lake. I understand now some portions of the trail are on high ground, but on this occasion you traveled the muskeg to get to winter fishing. A vehicle approached us coming from the lake; we pulled over and stopped. Our truck immediately got that sinking feeling, letting us know we had pulled over too far. It was early in the season and the only place it was frozen was on the well-traveled portion of the trail. The other truck tried to winch us out but had nothing to anchor to and broke his tow cable. The passenger side of the truck continued to sink until a quarter to half of the under carriage was high-centered. The only answer was for a small caterpillar to rescue us. Our radio was not working well; we needed Forestry to come out with a small cat.

And what to our wondering eyes did appear but a government helicopter. Observant as ever, the pilot saw our stressed-out vehicle and us standing around hoping the person who had originally tried to help us would talk to forestry.

The helicopter circled once landed. The pilot got out carrying a bag. We thought that was rather strange. As he approached we recognized him as a pilot who had flown us on patrols.

"This does not look too good. Who is on the way to get you out?"

My partner told the story of how we had gotten into this mess and sent for help.

"OK," said the pilot. "When I take off, I will radio Forestry and tell them the only thing that will get this truck out is a cat. They have a small one in Rocky that should do the job. Looks like you will be here for a while; you might as well have my lunch/supper and coffee. He gave us the bag he was carrying. Just leave the thermos at the office."

It was a kindness truly appreciated. We knew the request for help would get to the right place and we had food.

Now we waited. The cat came three hours later and rescued us after making the whole muskeg shake like a bowl full of jelly.

I had occasion to be on a forest fire as a bear control person. To ensure all the fire fighting crews and camps were free of bear interference, we spent a lot of time in helicopters. I expect to an experienced helicopter pilot the following is stressful, but not too.???

When flying in the helicopter we did bear work and Forestry work, as there was always staff from both disciplines on board. For reasons that I do not remember, on a number of occasions the forest officer requested the pilot to essentially park beside the top of the tallest spruce tree in the area so he could tie a colored ribbon on its very top.

This might not sound like much but consider the wind, the officer hanging out the door, and the time it takes to do the job, plus any movement in any direction will stop the tying operation immediately. Of course you realize the tree was on the opposite side of the helicopter from the pilot, partially blocked by the person tying the ribbon. Anyway each time was successful with only one try.

Psychology of the helicopter is not to be underestimated. Given time, as we sometimes were, an opportunity to surprise hunters with the ultimate patrol vehicle should never be overlooked. On one occasion south of High Prairie, in a clear-cut down towards the west end of the Swan Hills, just such an occasion arose.

For some time our office had been receiving complaints about illegal activity in that area day and night. Our vehicle patrols had not been able to locate any illegal activity. Lots of activity but all legal. What's that about? Our first chance this particular fall for a helicopter patrol was at hand. We knew exactly where to go.

On a frosty morning in late September, my partner and I met the helicopter at the High Prairie airport.

"Where do you want to go?" For some reason pilots always want to know that. It's probably better if they do. Pulling out my map with a tentative flight plan, I showed him the northwest corner of the Swan Hills.

"I haven't flown there before; it should be interesting. Anything in the area I should know about that might give us trouble?"

"Not as far as I know. It has been two years since I flew there in a fixed-wing. Something could have been built since then."

"OK, let's go," were the pilot's last comments as he headed for his side of the helicopter.

He started up, checked the instruments, and we were off.

I asked him to fly at about 1000 feet so we could have a look at hunting camps and hunter activity on the way. There were lots of hunters out. The problem when you are in the air is, for the most part, you cannot tell if infractions are being committed, unless you are flying an area completely closed to hunting.

Reaching our target area, I asked the pilot to go to 2000 ft and fly in a straight line for 3 miles; then we would move over and fly another line. The height would hopefully keep the hunters thinking we were flying over on our way to somewhere else and pay little attention to us. At that height we could still see activity on the ground well enough to give us an idea what the hunters were doing. On the first pass all we saw were hunters driving cut lines, a few walking. That's when they still had to wear red while hunting. On second pass we noticed a truck stopping, going a little way, stopping again, with someone periodically getting in and out of the truck. We hung back and watched for a few minutes. The behavior continued. I thought they might have been getting out to look at tracks but I couldn't tell from where we were.

I activated the radio mike.

"Is there any way we can get down there and surprise those hunters so they don't see us first?" I asked the pilot.

"From here it looks pretty rolling through that clear-cut they are coming up to. If we stay behind them and have a look at the terrain from a little lower, we can swing around either side of them out of their sight when they are going up a hill and be on the other side when they get there. With luck we'll be looking in the windshield from 50 to 100 yards when they come over the hill."

I just looked at him. That's a Game Warden's dream. No one gets to move without you seeing them. No trying to unload guns, no hiding booze, no taking rifles in from being out the window ready to shoot, nothing, no nothing.

"Did you hear that?" I said into the speaker, addressing my partner in the back of the helicopter.

"Sure did. I'm ready to go when we hit the ground."

I looked at the pilot and said, "Whenever you're ready."

He went lower, keeping back from our quarry, getting an idea of the terrain. A bank, sharp turn and our plan was in progress. Just skimming the treetops at the side of the clear-cut, we were behind another hill completely out of view from the truck going forward. Another turn took us back in the direction of the road. We swooped over the trees bordering the clear-cut, and there was the road the truck was on starting up the hill. Now we were at ground level heading for the road. Another bank and we were hovering, lined up looking up the hill for the truck. It did not come. We sat for what seemed like five minutes. The pilot looked at me I said, "Go!"

We started forward, gaining altitude slowly, 8 or 10 feet off the ground, rising as the hill rose. Barely underway, the truck appeared at the top of the hill. By now our windshield was even with the hilltop and the truck's windshield; we were about 30 yards away from the truck. Oh yes, the driver was still gripping the wheel. All you could see through the helicopter and truck windshields were open mouths and saucer-sized eyes.

To land safely the pilot backed off a little, but we could still observe any movement in the truck. There was none. My partner and I got out and went to the truck. The hunters were still sitting there, not saying anything.

"Good morning. Fish and Wildlife. Like to see your licenses please, and we'll check the guns," I said.

"Oh yeah, sure," was the driver's response, as he recovered from seeing something he hadn't expected.

"When did you guys start doing this? I never heard of helicopter checks on roads, only in camps. You scared the Hell out of us."

By now we had all the hunters out of the truck producing their licenses. My partner was checking the guns in the cab. He found three out of four loaded. Appropriate tickets were written.

The driver of the hunter's vehicle could not help himself.

"It was almost worth getting the tickets to see that helicopter appear out of nowhere. It was just like in the movies."

I always wanted to say this, and now was the time.

"Just doing our job spending your tax dollars."

He quit grinning. I thought maybe it was not such a good idea to say what I said, but it was true.

Try as I might, I never ever got in a position to have a helicopter perform the way that one did. That is the kind of thing that makes your day.

FLUSHER TRUCKS

"Flush" is usually associated with someone's complexion or your commode, but not in this story. Flush, in this context, has to do with washing paved streets in the City of Calgary, back in the mid 1950s when there weren't a lot.

An 18-year-old with mischief always in the back of his mind could not be happier than driving a 4-ton truck with a thousand-gallon water tank and a huge pump. It delivered water at up to 200 lbs per square inch through four nozzles. You can move and even break stuff with this kind of equipment and pressure.

There was minimal training provided, and I was approved to go. Each day the foreman would give me a list of paved streets to be washed (flushed) and I was off. The day would start by filling the water tank at the nearest fire hydrant.

Two nozzles were set to spray on the passenger's side of the truck, one at the right corner by the bumper spraying forward and to the side. One by the passenger door spraying towards the curb. The nozzles on the drivers side by the front corner of the bumper was set to spray the centre line and a little to the right. The other nozzle was left of. The nozzles were activated by levers on a panel easily within my reach. I was in business at 20 to 30 miles per hour, warning lights on. Small and large rocks were being propelled at flight speed in the general direction the water sprayed. Problem is they travel faster and farther and strike harder when they hit a stopped obstacle.

I quite liked this job. Once provided with my list of streets to flush for the day, I was on my own — quite independent for a city employee. You washed till you ran out of water, stopped at a fire hydrant, filled up with water and continued till you ran out of streets or quitting time came.

Gas-up had to be done at the end of each shift. On one of the trucks I drove, an esthetically correct hood covered the water pump motor mounted behind the cab. It was identical on both ends — radiator cap on one end and gas cap on the other. (Wait a sec; don't get ahead of me here.)

It was Friday afternoon and I was in a hurry. As I jumped out, somebody started to talk to me. I kept talking to them as I walked around the truck, checking things out for the next shift. I came to one end of the water pump motor, saw a cap protruding through the cover, climbed up, opened the cap, and stuck the gas nozzle in. I set the gas pump to keep running and jumped down to finish some last minute tasks. I no sooner hit the ground and the gas shut off.

What the heck? I climbed up again, started the gas; it shuts of again.

"Oh NO!" my mind screamed, the light coming on. "You dumb %&%^%*()&^%$$##!@. You just topped up the pump radiator with gas!" I mentally berated myself.

As it turned out, the mechanics agreed with my assessment. The hassling was relentless.

Anyway, the pump radiator was drained, refilled with antifreeze, and off I went, free to perform other mischief and mayhem, which didn't take long.

Despite the "radiator fiasco," I had proven myself a

responsible employee. When the new flusher trucks arrived I was given one to operate. No new training was required. "Just be careful of the nozzle pressure; it's higher on these new trucks," was the instruction I was given.

I was given the list of residential streets to wash (sounds better than flush) and off I went with my new truck, just like it was my own. Everything was going fine. Water pressure was a bit of an issue but it was quickly solved. I could not go any faster to complete my assigned tasks, but the new truck seemed to make it all easier and more fun.

About midmorning the foreman showed up, stopping in front of me. This was highly irregular. During the morning I had caught the odd glimpse of him in the rear-view mirror, but he never stopped. Something must be happening. I got out of the truck and walked over to his truck.

"Come on Chuck, we're going for a drive."

"OK," I said, wondering what this could be about as I walked around his truck to get in.

"Something wrong?" I asked as I closed the truck door.

"You'll see," was all he would say.

We turned around and went back over the street I had just washed. On previous occasions when I was involved in something that was not quite right I was told immediately. I could not imagine that I had done anything wrong. We traveled part of a block when he stopped.

He pointed at a house on my side of the street saying, "Take a look at the front of the house, about basement level."

It took a few seconds but I finally located what I thought he wanted me to see. This house had a basement window in front. There was a hole in the window with an accompanying spider-web shatter pattern in the glass.

I looked at the foreman. All he said was, "There's more."

We drove along my route with him pointing out almost every house with basement windows in front. Well at least there was consistency; they all had holes in them or were completely broken.

"So what do you think happened?" he asks.

I though he was supposed to be the smart one — after all he was the boss; he was the one who got paid to figure stuff out.

"It must have to do with the water pressure and the new sloped curbs. I had the pressure down as far as it would go and still wash the street."

"You are right. I was following you to see how the windows got broken. You probably could not see them but very small rocks were propelled by the water into the base of the sloped curb that apparently launched them at high enough speed to cross the lawns and still have enough power to break the basement windows."

"Did you see any windows break when you were following me?"

"No but I did see the rocks flying. Here is your new assignment for today: keep to all four-lane streets and avenues that have square curbs."

"Thanks. Sorry about the broken windows."

"Don't worry about it; stuff happens. I am in more trouble than you are for sending you out here. We did not realize the sloped curbs would cause that problem."

I waved went back to the truck and was off to my new assignment.

During the time I worked for the City of Calgary, I am not sure how much bylaw enforcement was done for "dogs running at large". As you may know, dogs have a need for entertainment, especially when running around on their own. For some reason, water squirting out of a nozzle at dog height from a truck going down their street was a challenge they had to deal with.

The dog would see me coming and run at the front nozzle, biting at the water. This in and of itself was not that bad, but sometimes the dog would not quit for a block or two. I had enough to do without watching out for someone's dog. I mentioned this problem to some of the old hands at the yard; they suggested a solution.

New day, new list of residential streets to wash and I was waiting for a dog. You guessed it: none showed up.

Finally, after coffee, here came the block bully charging at the front nozzle barking, snapping and growling. As instructed, upon seeing the dog I started cutting the pressure to that nozzle. By the time he got there, there was barley a trickle but still enough to keep him interested.

He continued to bark, growl and snap at the water. Now the time came: with a flick of the wrist, I applied maximum pressure to that nozzle.

"How the heck did that happen?" I asked myself, innocently.

The dog was soaking wet, on its side, lying on the sidewalk. I watched in the rear-view mirror. It got up slowly, shook itself off and went and sat on a nearby step. When I went back to do the other side of the street, guess who stayed on the step?

As a matter of interest, and to back up the claim about moving stuff, I will pass on some stories from the other drivers.

Warning signs were put up to advise residents that flusher trucks would be washing the streets at a certain time. When the flusher truck approached the rear of a parked vehicle, all nozzles activated, our instruction was to keep washing, as the car was parked where it was not supposed to be.

Just after passing the parked vehicle, the driver heard a thump on the passenger door. To his surprise there was a man running beside his truck with his face wet, hair dripping, banging on the door, yelling. Shutting off the truck and pump, the driver got out. By now the soaked man was at the driver's door threatening grievous bodily harm. Without going into the specific, sordid, details of the conversation, here's the rest of story.

Out of the truck driver's sight, the "resident" was lying under the car carrying out his vehicle repairs. As his feet were sticking out from under the front bumper, there was no chance for the truck driver to see him, as he had approached from the rear.

As the "civilized" discussion continued, neighbors started to appear as the truck driver and the "wet one" walked back to the vehicle repair site. What the truck driver observed was a toolbox, ratchets, open-end wrenches, and all other assorted tools, soaked and lying gleaming in the sunlight, strewn far and wide.

"Wet one" carried on about incompetent City employees and their bad eyesight; however, no bodily harm was done.

According to the driver, some of the neighbors really enjoyed their neighbor getting soaked.

DAM JUMPER

I am a big fan of water and boats. Fast water, slow water, lakes and rivers; it does not matter, I love them all.

When I was young, I was lucky enough to have a Dad who had a powerboat. It was mainly used on Gull Lake for waterskiing. However it did pique my interest in boats and how they operated. As a teenager, turning fast at high speeds was at the top of my list. Dad did not care too much for that, but what he did very well was, with unbounded patience, pull me around on my water skis. I think that's where my liking for the water started.

Working for Fish and Wildlife provided me ample opportunity to pursue my aquatic passion with abandon. As a Fish and Wildlife officer one will be in the water, on the water, or have something to do with water a good part of the time.

When I was at High Level there was all the water I could handle in the Peace River. Lakes were numerous, but few offered an opportunity for boating at that time. Fast water in the Peace River was interesting and in the spring, during flood times, there was debris from bank to bank. However, careful navigation would allow one to travel on the river, even when it was in that condition, with no problem.

In High Prairie my time was almost always on lakes, Lesser Slave being the biggest and most dangerous. In *POACHERS*

CRANBERRIES & SNOWSHOES and *POACHERS BEANS & BIRCH BARK*
there are stories about exploits on the water on and near Lesser Slave Lake. Other water stories are in *POACHER CHASER HOLIDAYS.*

At the west end of Lesser Slave Lake there is a bay called Buffalo Bay, fed by the Hart River, which is formed by the East and West Prairie Creeks. I had been checking for illegal nets in the shallows of Buffalo Bay and, not finding any, I decided that a trip up the Hart River to look for nets and to check trapping activity would be a good idea.

I was alone, operating a trusty government issue, 12-foot aluminum boat with a 9.9 horsepower motor. It did pretty well with one person on board. There was some minor flooding happening, so I had to pay attention and not be distracted by what might be a false branch of the river, otherwise I might find myself high and dry on the edge of a field.

Everything was going fine until a beaver dam appeared just as I rounded a bend. It was not very high, but prop-driven boats do not jump up very well at all, especially ones this small.

While coming upstream I had noticed significant water coming in from the west, a diversion I now surmised that was caused by the beaver dam. You guessed it. I wondered if I could get above the dam by taking the fast water I had seen. I backed off, turned around and found the fast water. My only concern with this side trip was hooking up on some unseen submerged object and flipping over. Well, you know the motto about the faint heart.

Off I went, full power, into a very narrow opening. What I had not seen from the main channel was the proliferation of willows that immediately shrouded the channel I had taken after the first small bend.

I had to stay under full power to maintain steerage. Getting pummeled by willows of an ever-increasing size was beginning to give me doubts about my decision. I was hunkered down in the boat as far as I could get and still be able to see to miss the large trees and willow bushes. I was amazed that the motor, even though it was on release, had not managed to hook up on something or that the propeller had not fouled.

Numerous thoughts and scenarios flicked through my mind but I had little time to dwell on any, as getting back to the river was my main concern. It seemed like forever, but before long there was a strip of water with little debris and no willows. A hard right turn got me into the river before I went into the bush on the other side. Did I mention the channel was not very wide?

Once I got my wits back about me and straightened out into the current I had time to think about where I ended up. I quickly concluded that the main channel was too narrow for me to safely continue upstream. If there were bad guys up there, too bad; they would have to wait for another day.

"Now how do I get turned around?" I wondered. The speed of the current and the little room provided to turn around combined to create a problem. Objects in water always want to go heavy end first (with the current). I had no intention of going backwards anywhere; that would be certain disaster. Boats will turn in their own length under full power. I had never done this where there was a current, so I could only hope for the best.

I fought my way upstream a little way to a slightly wider and longer open spot. Considering the length of the boat, the current, and the room I had to maneuver, this was the place to execute my turn. I went as far upstream as possible still maintaining as much maneuvering room as possible.

Maintaining idle against the current, I shifted my seating from the left side of the motor to the right to compensate for the current hitting the bottom of the boat in the turn. I then opened the throttle as far as it would go and jammed the motor hard left. The boat heeled over immediately so the right gunwale was just out of the water. As I shot through the turn, the current was helping hold the boat at a precarious angle, with some water now coming over the gunwale. Fortunately I was far enough around in the turn that I could straighten out and go downstream without swamping.

"What about the beaver dam?" you ask?

Well another reason I wanted to get far above the dam was so I could run the boat over it under full power. I'd seen it done on TV so there was no reason I could not do it.

Power on, I was heading downstream for the dam. In fact I was going fast enough I could cut back on the power just a little. Problem was I did not know exactly where the dam was.

I rounded a bend and saw water disappearing over the dam just ahead, only to re-emerge at the bottom of the dam, foaming and moving downstream.

Power on!!

The motor was already on release and the boat in a full plane when I felt the hull drag slightly as I crossed the water-covered dam. An eruption immediately followed as the prop jumped out of the water spinning in mid air at full rpm, screaming an "I must be in the water!" sound. One final "thump" every thing is back in the water and foam at the bottom of the beaver dam going down stream right side up.

"Now that was neat! A little scary — but very neat," I mused as I throttled back on the motor just as I approached the place I turned to go around the dam in the first place. The river was wider here so turning was not a problem. Turning back into the current, I thought, "Once is not enough; must make it two!"

Before starting the second run I checked the transom and motor to make sure nothing cracked or broke. Everything looked good.

On the second run I had a better idea where the dam was and that there were no obstacles between the dam and me. With full power from the get-go, the same chain of events took place as I went over the dam, although the motor whined about no water a little longer because of more power and more airtime. I also landed farther downstream.

"Now that was just fine!" I laughed, as I headed home.

Unfortunately, the conditions for that particular bit of mischief were never presented again.

LOST HUNTER

A career working in the great outdoors will at some time involve looking for a lost person. I had two experiences, the first one about a year after I started. We were patrolling southeast of Swan Hills early in the morning. Deer and moose season had just started. A vehicle came towards us quite a bit faster than usual down the bush road. We had a line of vehicles stopped checking licenses and what game had been taken. The road was very narrow you had to pull way over to let anyone pass. The developing scenario was causing us concern for everyone's safety. About three truck-lengths away the vehicle came to a skidding stop, turning sideways on the road.

"One of our hunters did not come back to camp last night. We knew you would not look till daylight for him. I was on my way to the nearest phone. He had breakfast yesterday and took a small lunch. We have not seen or heard of him since. I checked the other hunting camps on the way here, he is not at any of them and no one has seen him. Help us find him."

By now there were a number of hunters surrounding us listening to the talk.

"OK," said the boss. "We will help but some organization has to take place first." As he talked he got a map of the area out of our truck.

"This is the road we are on and now we should be about here. Where is your camp, and which way did he go?"

"I think our camp is about here," he indicated, pointing at a spot on the map.

"I can not be sure; this is my first time out here. But it's just a little ways back up the road. Let's go there." He indicated his friend had gone north from the camp.

"Just hang on a minute. Are the rest of you available to do a search when I get it organized? It should not take to long. I will go to their camp and be right back."

To a man they agreed to help.

We got in our truck and followed our somewhat harried hunter to the camp to see where it was and make sure the hunter had not come in the mean time. Upon seeing our uniforms, the camps hunters converged on us, all talking at the same time.

"Wait a minute," said the boss. "I need one person to tell me which way he said he was going. I already know when he left and how long he has been gone and he had no camping gear and did not plan to stay out overnight."

One man stepped forward and indicated on the map where the hunter said he was going.

"All we can hope for is he went where he said he would. By the look of access on the map, your camp is on the side of an upside-down triangle formed by cut lines and roads, with him walking into the center of the triangle to hunt. What we need to do is have people walk the sides and bottom — or in this case top — of the triangle, one starting at each of the three corners.

" I will organize you all to walk in a parallel line from one side of the triangle to the other as soon as I get back. I want to start him (pointing at me) walking the base of the triangle now, in case your friend starts to move and gets out of the triangle."

We walked to our truck. As we walked he said, "Did you bring your pistol?"

"Surely we're not going to shoot him if we find him?"

"No. Don't you ever quit? I am going to take you to the base of the triangle. You will walk the base till you get to where it hits the other side. Every three to five minutes while you are walking fire your pistol in the air. If he's within hearing distance, he will shoot his rifle if he has any shells left. In this fresh snow, you should easily be able to see if his tracks crossed the line you're walking. If they do, make a big arrow in the snow pointing which way you went. Got that?"

"Yes." We had arrived at my starting place.

"Wait, there is more. If you hear him shoot, walk towards the sound yelling his name. When you hear a response from him make sure you tell him you're from Fish and Wildlife and you have come to help him. He is going to have his rifle in his hands; we don't want that. Sometimes people, even though they have only been lost for a day or so, get mixed up. Take your lunch, and when you get close enough to recognize him and he sees your uniform, offer him a sandwich; he is going to be hungry. When he takes the sandwich, offer to hold his rifle so he won't have to put it in the snow. Let him have a few bites, then tell him we need to get going back to his camp; his friends are worried about him.

"This is important. He'll probably want to tell you how to get back to his camp. You tell him the only sure way to the camp is to follow your tracks in the snow, point them out to him, because you have just come from the camp. You got that so far?"

"When you're done I will repeat it back to you to make sure."

"There's an idea, so there's no mistakes. Here's the rest. Walk him back to where we are now and start walking down the road to the camp. You probably won't have to walk far because I am going to organize a road patrol to watch for him crossing the road, and with these big oilfield trucks going up and down the road I will ask them to blow their horns. The rest of them will be put in a line, and walk from one side of the triangle to the other yelling his name. One will have a rifle to shoot three shots in a row to signal he has been found so we can stop searching. Now tell me what you heard."

I repeated a Reader's Digest version back to him. He was pleased.

"That's good. If you don't find him come back here, by the look of the map and hills we know are here, that should take two to three hours. Most important, get his rifle as soon as you can. That close you will be able to have a good look at his eyes; if they have a vacant stare about them he is not as normal as he should be. Be careful; you can never turn your back on him; you can never tell what might happen. When you are walking out, make him go in front of you. Tell him you know he can follow tracks. Do not let him get behind you, ever!"

I opened the truck door and stepped out hearing him say, "Good luck and be careful. See you later."

I closed the truck door, put on my pack and started walking. While I was walking I took my pistol out of its holster and put it in my parka pocket for easy access. Down the line I went, thinking about all the stuff he had just told me.

At that time there was no prior training in search and rescue before you went into the field. This whole thing was brand new to me. What he said made sense. Remembering it all would be the trick.

I had 16 shells for my pistol. I would have to be careful how many times I shot. I walked for 5 minutes and shot one shot, stood and waited. No response kept walking. It was slow walking in the foot of snow with an inch or so of fresh snow on top. The up side, it sure was easy to see any fresh tracks. I was just getting ready to shoot again when I heard truck air horns. I waited there was another one. So he had gone back and asked the truckers to blow their horns along that part of the road, so the lost guy would know where the road was if he heard the horns. Sounds like a good idea. I shot, waited listened. No response.

I started walking again. As soon as I stepped into the snow I could not hear the horns anymore for the snow crunching. I carried on. Time to shoot. Shot. Waited. What was that? It sounded like a rifle shot, but I could hardly hear it. If it was a rifle shot, it came from where we thought he might be. I shot one more time. Waited, there it was again, barely audible.

I was sure he wouldn't be able to hear me but I yelled, "Stay where you are! I am coming to help you!"

With that I was off as fast as I could go towards the sound of the shot for 2 or 3 minutes. Hollered again that I was coming. No response. Fired the pistol in the air again. This time the sound of a shot was nearer and straight-ahead. I went in that direction for a couple of minutes, hollered again, listened. Still no response. I shot again. A response was almost immediate. Heading towards the sound for another 2 or 3 minutes, I hollered again. There was an audible response, barely. I yelled back, "Stay where you are! I am coming to help you!"

I followed the direction of the voice, then stopped again. "Where are you?"

"Over here," came from a grove of large spruce to my left. Sounded real close.

"Just stay there; I am coming."

Off towards the voice. I came around the base of some mature spruce and there he was 20 or 30 feet away, looking at me holding his rifle at the ready. "Hi, I am Chuck from Fish and Wildlife. Your friends were worried about you and asked us to come and help them look for you."

While talking I was taking off my pack and asked him if he was hungry and would like a sandwich. His rifle was lowered and he was within sandwich-grabbing distance in a heartbeat. Extending the sandwich I said, "Let me hold your rifle while you eat, so you don't have to put it in the snow."

In the other hand I had my water bottle and extended it to him. Now he would need both hands to hold food and water, making it easier for him to give up his rifle. There was no hesitation. He gave me the rifle; I gave him the water. We stood under the spruce trees while he ate the sandwich and drank some water. It struck me I could not hear the truck horns any more. Must be the thick spruce.

"You feel like starting for camp? You can have another sandwich while we walk." I was hoping this would get his mind off wanting to carry his rifle, and get us going.

"Sure we can go out the way I came here. I know how to get to camp." With that he turned and headed in the wrong direction.

" Hold on. Let's talk about this for a minute." He stopped I walked up to him.

"I just came here from the road and your camp. If we follow my tracks we will be sure to get to camp and the road. There will probably be a ride waiting for us at the road."

He was taking way too long to decide what he wanted to do encouragement was required.

"You have lots of bush experience; you can go first following my tracks that will get us to the road and your friends."

Thank goodness that persuaded him to start down the tracks I had made, still chewing the second sandwich and carrying the water.

"Are you sure this is the right way to go to camp?" he said, half turning towards me.

"You bet. You're doing a great job following those tracks; just keep going."

He kept on. It was not long till we hit the line I came in on. There was only one set of tracks for him to follow. They made a right angle turn towards the road. He followed without a word. A truck horn blared. He stopped.

"That was a truck horn; we must be close to the road."

"That's right. We will be there in a few minutes and get a ride to your camp."

It was not long and we could see the snow plowed up in a bank indicating the edge of the road.

"See the snow bank the road is right there," I said.

"I see it!" His pace quickened.

Just as we topped the snow bank a half-ton truck came along that was part of the search party. He pulled over and I explained we had located the person we were looking for and needed to take him back to camp. We piled in the truck; it was turned around and we were off to the camp.

There was a wide spot in the road where the search effort and camp were. It was jammed with vehicles. I spotted the boss, so we got out and headed for him. Turning, he saw us coming.

When we got to him he looked at the hunter then at me and said, "How's he doing?"

"He's much better now than before. He wants to see his friends; he did not want to worry them."

As I finished speaking some of his friends arrived, yelling his name and hitting him on the back. He went towards them. Happiness reigned supreme. Search successful, no injuries. A cold night alone in the bush was the main hardship.

Wrapping up the remaining questions, the boss officially turned the lost hunter over to his friends.

In the truck on the way home the boss asked,"What did you think of that?"

I was pleased to tell him every thing he told me before I got out of the truck turned out to be true. No all the other searchers are not still looking for the lost hunter. I did shoot my pistol three times to indicate the lost was found

The other search was also in the winter during hunting season, resulting in the successful location of the lost hunter.

TICK

Not the kind from a wind-up clock, nor the nursery rhyme. You already know. The blood-sucking, disease-carrying uglier-than-%^%^&* kind. A deadly Rocky Mountain spotted fever transporter. Pinning down the problem with the usual symptoms is difficult. Similarity between the fever and other common maladies is confusing. Without prompt attention you can die. There is no pre-bite immunizer.

Prevention is the only way. In this light, as usual, there are numerous suggestions. Light-colored clothing. Pants inside socks, sleeves done up tight, kerchief or bandana around the neck tight enough so you can feel these wonderful creatures crawl under it. They love hairy, warm places. Your head gives off 30 percent of your body's heat. If you have followed the previous directions on sleeves and pant legs, you should be OK. I don't need to remind you they are the routes to the other thermally dynamic areas of the body!

Observing hunters, hikers and other outdoor folks, you will rarely see the above behavior followed. They are all out at the bug's most active time.

Now to the tick story. My previous hunting partner, the guy I went hunting bears with on a pedal bike, and I decided a sheep hunt was in order. It was all arranged. Our camp was up Corral Creek about 2 miles from its confluence with the Kline River.

My partner had a ewe and a ram license. At that time the sheep population in that area was very high; it did not matter where you went, you saw them.

Two days we hiked around the numerous sheep trails covered with fresh sheep tracks, glassing every slope. Nary a sheep did we see. It figures. Finally, on the third day, a ewe was spotted on a rock outcropping, protruding from a mountain across the creek.

Fording the creek, our approach began. Breaking out of the trees some distance up the mountain, we saw our quarry, still standing where we last saw it. Problem was, it was nearly vertical to where the sheep was perched some 200 hundred yards away.

In order to take a shot, the shooter lay on the scree slope, his toes dug in as far as he could get them, elbows the same. The 300 magnum roared he was pushed back about a foot leaving deep groves in the scree from his elbows and boot toes.

Looking up slope all he and I could see was a sheep coming at him in a tumbling mass at unimaginable speed. Nearly vertical will do that. I hollered just as he rolled out of the way, ending up beside me. The sheep went tumbling past us about 40 yards and came to a stop against some bush.

Now where did the tick come from? Did I get it handling the sheep or pick it up off shrubbery along the trail? Ticks are hunters. They wait on foliage by trails with their grabbers ready to latch onto a meal. When secure, they ride along to see if it's fit for consumption — if not, releasing and waiting for another candidate.

After four days hunting it was time for a shower. Walking past the mirror in the bathroom I noticed a small, misshapen, and brown something between my shoulder blades. Must be a piece of stick thinks I. I tried to brush it off. To my surprise it did not move. Another try. No movement. Closer examination revealed it was a tick.

I tried freshly lit then blown-out wooden matches. Touching the tick's abdomen with the hot end of a match while looking over your shoulder into a mirror is tricky. I accomplished it a few times to no avail.

"Medical Clinic."

"Hi. I have a tick burrowed into my back between my shoulder blades and cannot get it off. It looks like it has some blood in it."

"Come to the clinic right now and we'll take it off."

"I've been in the bush four days and smell like a bear. I'll have a shower first."

"No. don't do that. You might break the head off the abdomen, leaving it in your back and difficult to remove."

"OK, I'm on the way."

Arriving at the clinic, I was ushered into a small room with an examination table, chair, sink, counter and wall cupboard.

"Let's have a look."

I took off my T-shirt and the nurse had a look.

"I'll get the doctor. You can lie down on your front; he'll be right here."

Moments later in he came.

"Let me explain what I have on the tray."

He held it down so I could see in my prone position.

A 5-inch by 5-inch by 1/8-inch thick piece of asbestos was to put on my skin under the tick, in case the doctor slipped with the heated paper clip soldered onto a pair of needle nose pliers. He would heat the paper clip with the Bunsen burner he lit with the cigarette lighter. The forceps were to pick up the tick if it came loose.

"Just lie down; this won't take long."

I heard him light the Bunsen burner.

I felt the cool asbestos on my back then nothing.

"I think it's dead; I'll have to cut it out."

"Oh, that sounds just fine. Go ahead."

"No, wait. The heat must have finally got to it. It's coming out. I have it. You can sit up now."

Sitting up, I came face to face with this nasty bit of work. To say I enjoyed seeing it squirm in the doctor's forceps would not be a lie.

"Would you like to kill it?"

He put it on the counter and I took great delight in squishing it.

"You need to wash your hands. Any contact, especially with the internal parts of these, can be dangerous."

"Thanks."

"Wait, the bite needs to be disinfected. Not only that, if you feel any symptoms of cold or flu with in the next two weeks come in right away. It could be Rocky Mountain spotted fever."

"Thanks once again."

I was into my T- shirt and out the door.

No Rocky Mountain spotted fever showed up.

TAR BABY

You are probably wondering what could be interesting about a truck that is used to oil streets in Calgary. Well sit back; you are in for a surprise. Before the surprise you need to know the oil deposited on the gravel roads in Calgary in the 1950s smelled a lot like crude oil and looked the same: black, thick and sticky.

After you acquired some experience in the use of other trucks and were found to be somewhat dependable, you might be offered the job of an oil truck operator. It was a rather prestigious position, as truck-driving positions went. You spent a lot of time keeping the cab of the truck clean in and out. They even gave out wax for the outside of the cab. I must admit, that red 4-ton looked special all shined up.

So the grader scarifies (digs up the top 6 inches of gravel), puts it in a windrow, and you drive over the windrow, saturating it with oil. The grader turns the windrow over and you saturate again. This continues till the foreman says enough. Now the grader spreads the windrow out in equal thickness all over the road surface. It is your turn again. You get to give it a final soaking before departing.

The oiling procedure is all done at slow speeds, 5 to 10 miles per hour. It must be the smell of the oil or just maybe the shiny red truck that causes the trouble, but it comes.

I was attempting to lay down even strips of oil to cover the width of the road when I noticed just ahead a calico cat running across a lawn, directly towards a part of the road I just oiled. It made it to mid-road when it realized something was wrong. I figured everything was OK; the cat was a distance ahead but in my line of travel. One must not deviate! The cat had stopped dead, lifted one front paw, looked at it, put it down, lifted a rear paw, shook it, put it down. I was getting within spitting distance and not about to turn or stop. I saw the other rear paw come out of the oil and start to shake, just as the hood of the truck obscured my view of the cat.

That's when I activated the cat behavior modification device. The cat was in overdrive, spraying oil and gravel right to the far curb and making perfect black oil cat tracks at each bound up its owner's sidewalk. Air horns are wonderful!

Sometimes parents are not as mindful of their toddlers as they should be. We're talking kids who are between the crawling and I-can-almost-walk-on-my-own stage. That's when they can barely walk, but can crawl at what is warp speed to their parents. They were here and now they're gone. You would think after all the noise from the grader digging up the road and the trucks going back and forth, folks would be watching their kids, or at least come to see why it got mausoleum-quiet before letting them loose. A single truck oiling a road at 10 miles per hour after the previous activity is silence.

Well, they do not always check; that's why there is a story. As previously, I was doing the final oiling when down the block appeared a toddler on the lush green grass of July. This little diaper-clad person was barely able to stand on its own, but was making a Herculean effort to walk to the front sidewalk and the freshly oiled road. About halfway across the lawn, leg power gave out. A diaper starting to come down may have contributed.

Now it was warp speed for the sidewalk on all fours. Interestingly, no parents had appeared yet. There was no slowing down whatsoever on the mission heading for the sidewalk. I should let you know here that I do stop for small children. No worries. At the curb all forward motion stopped. The diaper had continued the downward slide, so there would be no walking. Observing the moving black creek only inches away in the gutter, can you imagine the joy in the mind of a child with no one to say, "Don't do that; don't touch."

"It looks like where Mommy takes me to play; it's just a different color, but it moves. I have to touch it." Not quite able to reach from the all-fours position, a prone position was reached. One hand went to the moving black liquid, then the other. Splash, splash. It was just like the bathtub — what fun! Wet and warm. It was a little slippery and smelled different, not like the bath water. "I need to try a taste. I'll lick my finger." I was close enough to see the facial expression. It was, "Yuk it tastes terrible!"

Having been fortunate enough to observe all this mischief, you can imagine my warped sense of humor going wild at what would happen when a caregiver finally showed up. I was almost parallel to the previously diaper-clad child that was quickly turning into a tar baby, head, chest, back, face and hair covered. Continuous gleeful splashing in the lukewarm crude oil will do that for anybody. Hysterical screaming accompanied a woman in overdrive who appeared from beside a house behind the toddler. No reaction from our black oil-soaked toddler.

Next question: how does one pick up a child soaked in crude oil? I was about to see. There was no hesitation. Words of disparagement towards herself and the child were heard, accompanied by her bending over, taking the errant toddler under the arms, lifting it straight in front of her and bringing it towards her chest. "Ah," I thought, "a dedicated mother; nothing matters but the child." Not quite true! She had turned the oily one to face her while picking it up, finally seeing the extent of the oil bath. The oily one was now sharing just like mom taught. Crying, screaming, kicking and arm-flailing had spread oil to mom. She was bringing the child close to her chest when something happened. Was it the smell of the crude or the sticky, slippery, blackness of the oil? I will never know. The child was held at arms-length still screaming and sharing as they disappeared around the corner of the house.

I was surprised there were no disparaging words, not even a glance of condemnation, at the oil truck. Oh, by the way, no call to City Hall either.

GRIZZLY BEARS AND TEA

We had been waiting for the weather to get nicer for a hike in the mountains. That was happening. Now the question was where to go. There are so many places to choose from. We finally decided on the Kline River and Coral Creek Canyon.

Parking the truck on the north side of the Kline River at the staging area, we started our hike along the old seismic trail paralleling the north bank. Just out of the staging area, we picked our way across a wet spot caused by a continuously running spring of very good water, a drink of which was much appreciated after a hike or hunt. From there it was up a south-facing cut to the wide trail that was sometimes flat, sometimes sloped to the south. There was lots of horse sign, both tracks and road apples. Careful scrutiny of the trail also revealed deer, elk and bear tracks.

The long, relatively straight piece of the trail ended when it came to the east bank of the junction of Coral Creek and the Kline River. Then there were two choices: continue on to the trail paralleling the Coral Creek Canyon, or follow the well-established trail just to the east of that, where most human traffic and horses went. We chose the trail along the canyon. The narrowness of the creek and height of the canyon walls made continuous viewing of the water from the top of the canyon impossible.

Some years ago an ardent gold prospector parked his camper at the staging area and, leaving his wife behind, he hiked it to the canyon. He was convinced, as are all prospectors that gold will be in the most difficult places to access. With that in mind, he located a place on the canyon wall to lower himself down to water level to have a look for gold and do a little panning. He was successful in getting to the bottom of the canyon. After having a look around where he ended up, he soon came to the realization that he could not go up or downstream because of high, fast water flow and vertical rock banks. Attempts to get out of the canyon the way he entered were futile. Day was ending. It looked like he would have to stay in the cold damp canyon overnight.

As darkness fell, his wife got concerned. She, with assistance of others, notified the authorities, who advised they would undertake a search at first light. It was far too dangerous to search canyons in the dark of night.

At first light the search crews located where he went into the canyon and lowered themselves down to find the man cold, shivering and hungry, but none the worse for wear. He was assisted out of the canyon and back to his wife, hopefully to prospect another day. As far as I know no gold was found.

We continued our hike along the edge of the canyon to where it back slopes from the vertical banks into wonderful winter sheep range. The sheep range has its own little valleys running back to a trail at the top of the bank. Sheep have worn a trail along the top of the widened canyon, making it easy walking and opening up the view so you can see the mountain panorama on the other side of Coral Creek. This trail eventually meets the trail for horses and people on top of a hill. We stopped to admire the panoramic view of the Coral Creek river flats, where elk are often seen, with mountains on the other side stretching up to reach the White Goat Wilderness area boundary.

Sheep could be seen across the creek, high on the slopes above the treeline, grazing contentedly. No other wildlife was visible — very unusual. We started down the trail to the river that was, over time, becoming narrower and narrower due to sloughing of the fine soil and loose rock. At the bottom of the hill we took a side trip along the far east edge of the river flat, where the original river bank would have been. A short distance to the north there is a shear rock wall running north, with a cut in it coming from up the mountain. As it goes into the rock it widens out. There are rumors that, in the days of hippies, some resided in this nondescript lair for a time. I am guessing summer only, if at all. It did not look that homey. That may have changed with access to mind-altering drugs.

From there we went back across the horse trail that runs the length of Coral Creek to Job Pass and beyond. An abundance of wildlife and spectacular scenery make this trail a favorite of hikers, horseback riders and outfitters. Crossing it, we made our way to the creek bank, took of our boots and socks and waded across. It is not very wide — 20 to 30 feet, depending on run off. It makes up for this by being very cold on the bare legs and feet, making them numb in a hurry. Using a walking stick to steady yourself against the current and to move rocks is helpful. We got across and followed an animal trail up one of the bald hills at the creek's edge. It led to a navigable rock face, terminating in a short scree slope part way up the mountain that forms the east boundary of the White Goat Wilderness area. Having navigated this, we followed our trail into a gully, eventually ending in a saddle, from the top of which was a view nothing less than spectacular. Snow-capped mountains on all sides and the glacial blue of the Kline River accented a kaleidoscope of blues, greens and whites. A view unaltered by the human hand.

We were on the edge of the wilderness area that extends to the national park in the west. Lunch and a drink of water were in order. With no safe place to make tea, that would have to wait. As we sat eating our lunch, admiring the never-ending vista of mountain scenery, sheep and mule deer came within yards until they realized we were there, then bounded off. Our minds awash with the incredible scenery, it was time to go.

Making our way back the way we had come, we arrived at the bald hill just above the creek. Stopping for a look around to see what might be next, we saw a grizzly bear across the creek just above the river flats sniffing around. You guessed it. It's activities were taking place right where we had walked to get where we were. It was obvious after some observation that it was in no hurry, and now neither were we. It was slowly making its way to the creek near where we crossed.

Unfortunately, there are few ways out of the river valley at this point, due to the height and nature of the terrain. Our strategy was to continue down the bald hill to the creek and make tea on a gravel bar. One last look at the bear and its slow, continuous progress in our direction and we were off. It was about half a mile away the last time we saw it before we went into the bush.

At the creek we found a suitable place to make tea, gathered wood, got out our vintage tea pail, blackened from way too many fires, set it in the coals of the fire and waited for the water to boil.

Our interest was in the direction the bear might come from as we sipped our tea. After two cups of tea we decided it was time to make our way to the base of the hill where the trail went up. If the bear was still around it should have been between our fire and the base of the hill. It was fairly open through here so there would be no surprises for bears or people. There weren't. The last we saw of the bear was from the bald hill. We did see grizzly tracks, on the trail at the base of the hill in the dirt and gravel just before you start up, probably made by that bear.

I have never been on any trails in that area without seeing fresh bears tracks. The only time they make me nervous is when, after I have been walking for a while, all of a sudden there are fresh bear tracks coming towards me and no bear to be seen. Where is it? Watching me from somewhere very close? Probably. Watching is good. Keep walking and watching; you don't have much choice.

Another adventure.

DISSERTATIONS ON RELIEF

To say people have strange habits is, we all know, an understatement. This story will illustrate one of the strangest ones I ever ran across. First a little background.

Since I was a toddler I have been involved with things to do with outhouses. Not because I wanted to, just because it happened, kind of like why you use one. It comes naturally.

My first experiences in this area were at Gull Lake in Alberta. The outdoor facilities were just down the hill from the cabin. The 10-yard trail to the commode had very tall overhanging Saskatoon bushes on both sides. Excellent for spiders and their ilk. When I was at the cabin with my aunt and cousin, one of my jobs was to be the first one to the outhouse in the morning. It was pointed out by my aunt that I was the best cobweb destroyer she had ever known. Having spent a good many of her younger years using one of these facilities, I am sure she knew what she was talking about.

Little boys even at eight or ten have an abundance of mischief genes. (They could be blue!) It was not long before the morning ritual of spider web removal got a little boring. Besides, I observed on a few occasions the fuss when she had to be first. It was quite a show: arms flailing, some loud descriptive words about spiders and general aggravation caused by the webs getting on her face in her eyes and on her clothing. Of course the odd spider would be on the destroyed webs, and in desperation attach itself to what ever it could find — usually Aunty. As she settled in for a comforting repose in the single-holer you may have heard a cacophony of sound, unintelligible, except for the derogatory terms directed at some poor misguided spider whose desperate attempt to save himself got him a ride into an outhouse with a spider-hater.

I digress for a moment to tell you about Aunty and a real spider story. My dad (her brother), my mother and I were at the cabin together. Aunty suffered periodic bouts of migraine headaches. One was taking place now, her misery obvious. Relief was in the form of retreating to the nearest dark bedroom and lying down. The family summer cabin where we were staying was very small, with two bedrooms big enough to hold a bed and small dresser, no more. The bed was against the wall on one side. Just a curtain hung over the doorway, and walls went halfway to the roof.

"Please bring me some water," came a weak voice from the bedroom. Dad was on the way, filling a glass from the dipper in the water pail for Aunty.

As he opened the curtain I went in beside him to see how Aunty was doing. She sat up in the semi-darkness. The single coal oil light in the main room was the only lighting for the whole cabin. Leaning on one elbow, she took the glass of water from Dad. Remember, nine-year-olds do not take up much room. Being small and working in the semi-dark, I was able to get next to the doorjamb and into the room when she had her head up drinking. That's when I brought out my new pet. A tarantula. With great dexterity I placed it on the white pillow in the depression where her head had been. It looked enormous. I ducked out under the curtain into the next room. She thanked

Dad for the water. He came out with the empty glass; a look on his face that I would later learn was the "this should be good" look. He had seen everything I did. One step from the curtained doorway, his ears and everyone else's were assailed with a scream that loosened the knots in the cabin walls and floorboards. No words, just a scream.

Small but fast and afraid of loud noise, I was out the door in three steps, letting it slam behind me. There was no pursuit. Dad was talking to Aunty, who finally realized it was a rubber spider.

"You did that? What's wrong with you? When we were kids you did that stuff to us! You're 50 years old; it's time to stop!" Never a word did he say.

"Wait a minute! Chuck did that, didn't he? Sure he did; I remember seeing him. Why didn't you stop him? Be careful; he will turn out like you."

I guessed she lay back down because I heard the bedsprings squeak. I was standing outside when Dad came out with his pipe going. He walked over to me and said,

"You should have more consideration for your aunt when she has a headache.

You need to apologize to her for scaring her so bad. She thought it was a real spider."

"OK." I started for the door.

"Just a minute. That was not a bad joke, but be careful when you do that stuff; people may want to get even."

That was quite a digression, but those father-son bonding stories need to be told.

Back to the story proper. Outhouses and their necessity are well known. While employed with seismic in the Arctic, volunteers were asked to build an outhouse. I was front and center. Hand-sawn lumber and nails were at hand. Eventually two of us got to work. A single hole outhouse is not a major construction project. The size of the project was small but the immediacy of completion was large. The party chief wanted it completed within a day due to the free-ranging fertilization efforts of the crew whenever the internal urge of movement came upon them.

Construction commenced immediately in the -30 F weather. It was not long and the walls were built. It was a prefab outhouse. Walls, roof, floor and door complete, the most important part was next: the throne. Reposing in your time of need requires a degree of comfort under all circumstances. Body measurements were taken to ensure proper seat height. No one wants anything to be left dangling while cogitating!!! The seat's framework was complete. Proximity and size of the used food receptacle opening and its proximity to the seat front is critical.

Even north of the Arctic Circle, a quiet moment of repose at -40 F should be enjoyed in comfort. With the appropriate marks on a piece of plywood, we commenced to cut a hole. It was in two pieces of plywood we split so we could saw half the hole in each half, then match them up and nail everything down. Our only saw was a standard carpenter's crosscut saw. We were able to get more of the customary oval shape cutting the board when it was in two halves than in one piece. This accomplished, we set the seat boards back on the seat frame and field-tested them for comfort. The receptacle hole board was designed to move back and forth till we determined an ideally comfortable location for the hole from the front of the seat. We did this fully clothed, as there were lots of splinters you know where. A lack of sand paper gave us a problem finishing the edges of the hole. We did the best we could with a hatchet, pocketknives and a rasp.

A cat made a hole for the many anticipated deposits we felt would be made. No, no, a real cat with tracks and a winch. We customized the hole with shovels and lumber to level the commode. There would be no odor; deposits were frozen immediately, just like when you misbehave with your bank account.

Before we get to the real reason for this whole chapter I must tell you (like you did not already know) there was precious little entertainment other than movies and reading. For those who did not care to patronize the new commode, another form of entertainment developed.

Pants unbuckled, roll of toilet paper over two fingers of the non-wiping hand, you waited till the timer said go. Out the door, around to the back of the bunkhouse, deposit, wipe, pants up back, into to bunkhouse. Time was recorded. I think our best time for those who participated was one and a half minutes. Somehow after the party chief got his outhouse, his concern over the free-rangers disappeared. He left us alone.

A story yet untold that would only take place in the Arctic is where I tried to start with this diatribe and where I will end. A member of the recording crew had peculiarities. He was not a free-ranger the party chief did not care for. He was not a patron of the newest establishment on the block that collected used, unwanted deposits. His thing was unique.

After we arrived at our daily worksite, he would gatherer some small sticks from along the cutline and make a small fire at the side of the cutline. His work would continue for a few minutes while the fire got as big as it could get, considering the fuel. When the fire was at just the right temperature, he would approach it with great satisfaction and apparent expectation, this while in the throws of disrobing from the waist down.

Heavy outer garments out of the way he was now by the fire. The wind dictated which side of the fire he crouched on; he crouched close because the fire was small. If we noticed a change in wind direction while he was doing his business we all looked. I know you have to be a little weird to get a kick out of some guy crow-hopping around a fire, trying to keep his butt from getting singed, or frozen. He was otherwise very well mannered, and always kept his bare behind to the snow bank on the side of the cutline. Interestingly, he would remain crouched by his little fire until it burnt down to nothing.

By now we were ready to move to our next location, business and entertainment complete.

Dissertations on defecations of delight?

SEAMIER SIDE

New on the job, we're all keen to do the best we can. This assignment was on a different order for my boss and me. The moose population in the Swan Hills in the late 50s and early 60s was deemed to be too high. How to solve this biological dilemma was the problem. Evidence was clear: All the bush moose liked to browse had been eaten down till it looked like the bristly end of a corn broom. Clearly there was not enough winter food for the moose. The other problem was the wolves. They're appeared to be lots and they were taking some moose. The government of the day wanted the moose population to remain the same or go up so hunters would have more success. The answerer seemed obvious. Get rid of the wolves.

We were assigned to thin out the wolf population to help the moose population. There is one sure way to do that. It is with something we do not like to use but its effectiveness outweighs the down side: strychnine. It is a common poison used in many applications.

A plan was formulated. As mentioned in another story, we hired a professional trapper with his expertise and equipment to work with us. We all went on a helicopter patrol to locate the heaviest concentrations of wolves. Without the helicopter patrol, we were pretty sure where most of the wolf packs were from hunter and trapper information and personal observation. Helicopter confirmation would be good. We took off on a bright, crisp winter day for the Swan Hills. We mapped out a grid pattern on an area map so we could reference our position and record pertinent information for future use.

During the flight, we confirmed our previous information on pack location, and selected locations to set the bait. We also looked for deadfall and hills on our route to a bait site. All the information was marked on the map.

We arranged to meet a few days later to discuss our first trip to set the bait. During that time we made up strychnine pellets. These consisted of a 1-ounce paper cup half filled with liquid lard. It was partially cooled and a 1/8" x 1/8" strychnine cube inserted. The remainder of the cup was filled with lard; then the whole thing was allowed to cool. We made lots.

The draw bait, as it is called, would be a hindquarter of moose. We had moose meat seized during the previous hunting season that was freezer burnt and not fit for human consumption. It was just what we needed.

Everything was ready; a date was set. We had two of those newfangled machines called Skidoos to get all the paraphernalia to our chosen site. These machines were the double track variety, allowing maximum buoyancy on the feet of snow present, plus great pulling power to get the bait- and equipment-laden toboggans in and wolves out when required. Top speed: 7 to 10 miles per hour. Much faster than snowshoes. We had two Skidoos and two toboggans.

Loaded, off we went. Going down the trail we saw marten, weasel, lynx, coyote, moose and deer sign, but no wolf sign on our way to our bait site. Arriving at the bait site, we saw very fresh wolf tracks crossing the lake on the way to its center, where the bait would be located. A hole was chipped in the 3-foot thick lake ice about 10 inches across till water bubbled out. The weight of snow on the ice caused minor flooding in the immediate area because it relieved pressure on the water from the ice allowing water to come up through the hole we made. Not serious. The hole completed, we unloaded the quarter of a moose and put the hoof in the hole in the ice. It went in far enough to freeze in the bony part of the moose leg, which was what we wanted. No wolves would get it loose. Next we cut slits in the exposed moose meat where 1/8-inch square strychnine cubes would be inserted, and the meat pressed back over the slit.

About 20 to 30 feet away, we made waist-high snow mounds, about six in number, in a circle around the frozen in moose quarter. In these snow mounds we placed three to six 1-ounce baits with lard and strychnine in them, minus the paper cup. One of these was sufficient to kill a wolf.

The theory behind this is the dominant wolf will come to the moose leg, eating off it and defending it from the rest of the pack. While they wait for their turn to eat, the rest of the pack will smell the lard in the snow mounds and gulp it down. I wondered how efficient this would be. Someone else had obviously used it and been successful.

Time would tell. It was dark when we finished our work, so we headed for the trapper's cabin at the east end of the lake. We had permission from the trapper to stay there for the night.

On the way to the cabin we stopped and made another hole in the ice so we could catch fish for supper. While the cabin was being opened and a fire made, fishing went on. It was not long and we had two 3-pound Jacks — just enough for supper. Approaching the cabin I could see light from the cabin reflecting off the snow and the smoke rising out of the chimney. A full moon rising over the cabin was painting the landscape an icy winter white, ensuring I knew it was winter and cold. It all looked like a postcard.

A blast of hot air from the stove hit me right in the face when I opened the door. It was a treat after the cold of the day. Our catch had been cleaned at the fishing hole and was handed to the designated supper cook. A frying pan with hot oil was already on the stove, awaiting the fish's arrival.

"You were right about the color of the fish's meat; it does have a pinkish tint to it," said the cook.

"The trapper told me all the fish he caught out of this lake had that color meat and they tasted better than Jacks from other places," replied my boss.

"Some of the trappers who have lakes on their traplines with Jacks noticed every time the Jacks have pinkish meat those things called fresh-water shrimp are in the lake. I don't remember seeing any when we made the holes in the ice, do you?"

We both answered "No," and watched while the rest of supper was prepared: warmed-up canned vegetables with bread and butter. After the first few bites of the freshly caught and fried fish, there was nothing but praise for the cook, and how they were still Jacks, but none had ever tasted like this. Canned fruit for dessert.

Next morning dawned bright and clear, and we were homeward bound.

To ensure maximum efficiency of this project, a check schedule for our bait was established at once every two weeks. That is generally the length of time it takes a wolf pack to cover its home territory.

In two weeks we returned to our bait site. We could see from afar, covered with new snow, eight humps near our bait on the lake's otherwise white, pristine surface. We had taken eight wolves. Their body heat had frozen them into the snow-covered ice. Freeing them, we discovered they appeared to be all adults. They were loaded into the toboggans for the trip home where they would be thawed out, skinned, hides sold at the fur auction, with monies going to general revenue.

To ensure no species was taken other than wolves, this project was only carried out in the winter, when a limited number of predators are about and you can secure the bait in a place large enough you can find the affected wolves. I was amazed no coyotes ventured out to the bait; none were seen or poisoned. It was all cleaned up and burnt prior to the return of spring.

None of us liked what we were doing. Dealing with poison is a disconcerting business to say the least. At the time it was thought to be the best solution to a perceived problem.

We left the bait at the same location for the total project; the theory being when a wolf pack moves on another will come to take its place. That must be true; they just kept coming.

Wolf numbers taken during two winters of this activity were enough to show some interesting characteristics. Wolf appearance varied from a Labrador retriever look to a German shepherd look. This was most pronounced in the short Labrador muzzle on some and the longer German shepherd-looking muzzle on others. They all had one thing in common: red or maroon hair between their toes.

While looking at some wolf skins ready to go to the fur auction I noticed something I thought was unique.

"Hey boss, how come these wolves all have had maroon or red hair between their toes?"

He looked at me and never batted an eye answering.

"I thought you would have figured that out by now; it's

from running through the cranberries."

We laughed. That was the best reason I got. Maybe it's true.

The government finally realized our efforts were not the answer to the moose problem to many moose were.

DRAG RACE

1958 Ford, 4-ton, single-axle dump trucks, the vehicle of choice. These were the standard truck for the City of Calgary back in (yes, you guessed it) 1958. Another time when the jobs outnumbered the labor force. Job recruiters were at the high schools looking for summer workers.

I had worked for the city for two or three summers by then. That got me a position on the afternoon shift, 4 p.m. to midnight. This shift was desirable because it paid more than the day shift — only a few cents, but it all helped. In case you are interested, the pay rate in the late 50s for truck driving was in the range of $1.50 to $1.75 per hour — princely sum compared to what my friends were making.

When it rained we were given a list of streets and avenues to drive to clean the catch basins. Catch basins are the grilled pieces of metal, about 16 inches square, you see on every corner that liquid running down the gutter disappears through. Debris, such as paper, cloth, etc., collects on the catch basin, rendering it useless by stopping the water flowing into it. The debris we loaded into the back of the trucks.

There was also gravel and asphalt to be hauled and stockpiled for maintenance and road building. Stockpiling gravel is not very exciting. You drive from the gravel pit to the gravel pile, drive up the pile, back up and dump your load over the side of the pile and go back for more. Well, stuff happens.

Late in the afternoon, with quitting time in sight, I was dumping my last load. I'm still not sure what happened, but I reached out and back through the open window to pull the rope activating the tailgate so it would open and let the gravel out. The pile was about 20 feet high. I felt the truck lurch back when it was not supposed to. I knew I had backed off the pile. The rest of what happened is a blur.

I was very quickly out the door. Maybe ships' captains go down with their ships, but I was not going down with my truck.

Five steps later I stopped to see what had happened. The truck was still there. How could that be? The answer soon became evident. The truck was solidly supported by the edge of the gravel pile pressed against the frame from just ahead of the back wheels to the back of the cab. It was going nowhere.

I realized I could not do anything myself so I walked down the gravel pile to the shop, all the time watching to see if the truck stayed put. It was still in place when I went through the shop door.

When the door opened the guys that were standing around stopped talking, apparently to see who was coming in.

"What are you doing here? I thought you were piling gravel."

"I was, but I have a problem."

"What happened? Did you back the truck of the pile?" They all laughed.

"Well, kind of," I said.

"Holy crap! Why didn't you tell us? You look OK. What happened to the truck?"

"The truck is OK. It is hung up on the edge of the pile on the frame, with the load still on."

"Come on," said the loader-operator, going out the door. "There is no telling how long it will stay there. That gravel is not very stable."

The rest came to the door to have a look but could have cared less. I was glad it was still where I had left it.

"What's the best way to get the truck down?" I asked.

"You may not think this now, but you are not the first guy who has done this. You were lucky; lots of times the trucks go over backwards tumble to the bottom of the pile and injure the driver.

"I was thinking about that. I leaped out of the truck as soon as it felt like it was tipping over backwards and I had no control of it."

"Wise decision. I am going to get the loader; meet you on top of the pile."

"Now what is he going to do with the loader?" I wondered.

I watched him drive up the pile and, to my surprise, I saw a long heavy chain in his bucket. It came to me in a flash. He will use the loader for an anchor so the truck will not go backwards off the pile when we unload the gravel.

He pulled up in front of the truck with the loader. I got the chain out of the bucket hooked one end to the bucket frame and the other end to the truck frame. He got the chain banjo string tight, shut the loader down and set the brakes. Getting out of his machine he grabbed his shovel from its holder on the machine came towards me said, "Get your shovel. This is payback for backing off the pile. We have to shovel the gravel off because if you lift the box the loader and truck may both go for an unexpected ride."

We climbed in and started shoveling. I think that single-axle, 1958 Ford 4-tons had a 4- or 5-yard box. Nothing by today's standards. It was not that hard shoveling; it seemed like no time when I heard, "That should be good. You get in, start it, put it in second gear. I will signal you when to start driving."

He turned for his loader as I was getting in the truck. By the time he started up I was waiting. The loader belched black smoke and I felt the truck move forward. He signaled I let out the clutch and did my favorite thing: give it gas. He was backing up and I was moving forward. What a relief. The truck was now on solid gravel. The chain was unhooked.

"Thanks."

"Not to mention it. You're not the first, nor will you be the last, but probably one of the luckiest."

I backed up very carefully and dumped what was left of my load. With that we got in our units and drove down the pile. It was a quitting time.

When you hire workers you expect them to do the best job they can, given the equipment you provide — a reasonable expectation. However, on occasion, the employee may want to test the new equipment to ensure it meets his or her satisfaction. From my standpoint, power, in the way of pulling and speed, are important criteria for trucks.

The 1958 Fords previously spoken of appeared to measure up. They had power and speed, said management — plenty of both for in the city. You know that is not even close to a satisfactory answer to the curious and free-spirited.

In that light, those of us on afternoon shift decided some private testing was required. The only place we could run abreast like a racetrack was on the new one-way streets in downtown Calgary. One-way streets were new to Calgary in the late 1950s, and appeared to be an ideal place for testing. It runs in my mind the one-way streets of the day were three lanes wide, and all in the downtown area.

"Who has the fastest truck?" that was the question. Those who were interested arranged to be downtown near the end of our shift, because at that time Calgary almost shut down after midnight.

Arranging our units three abreast we would all be at a red light together. On the orange light the trucks were put in second gear, clutch slightly released a little pressure on the gas pedal. Green! We were off, pedal to the metal, shifting gears as fast as we could. It was quite a rush racing three abreast on a downtown street, changing gears as fast as we could. First one would be ahead, then another. Our abilities such as they were, everything seemed to be about even. On a few occasions you had time to look around. There was the odd person who stopped to see what all the noise was about and why three trucks with City of Calgary on them would be doing what they were doing.

We were careful not to do this too often and attract undue attention, but it was fun while it lasted

BANG

Seismic work requires dynamite of one type or another, some times called "Geo-Gel," to be exploded at a certain depth down a pre-drilled hole at a specified location. This work is all part of a master plan to obtain a geophysical record of the earth's strata, to determine the likelihood of petroleum deposits in a given area. The recording is accomplished by using a geophone, an armature in a 2-inch by 2-inch metal cylinder with a base, having three short, downward-facing metal prongs. The geophones are put into the snow or muskeg on a seismic line, and connected to a common conductor cable running in either direction from the recording truck. The geophones and cable may stretch from a quarter to a third mile from the recording truck, which is situated in close proximity to the hole where the dynamite is loaded and detonated.

There is sometimes an array of holes in a line, usually with the one by the recording truck up to 300 feet deep or even deeper. The rest, however many there are, may be different depths. Proximity of holes, depth and amount of explosive per hole are predetermined before the seismic program begins.

The "shooter" (the man responsible for loading the holes) follows the drillers, and when they have drilled a hole he loads the appropriate amount of explosive. Loading holes in the permafrost is easy, because gravity takes the explosive down the hole complete with blasting cap and lead wire for detonating the charge. In all other situations, drilling mud is used to lubricate the drill as it progress down the hole; hence the explosive charge must be pushed through it. In permafrost, the friction caused by the drill provides enough lubricant by melting the permafrost for drilling, hence no drilling mud.

On occasion, when the holes are drilled, groundwater is present. In these cases the explosive has to be pushed down the hole with loading poles. Usually the shooter does not find out about these holes till suppertime. They have to be loaded for the next day's work and before the water in them freezes. No one wants to go back out in the dark after supper and pound back over the seismic lines to load holes you would be going to the next day. However, for safety reasons, no one went out in a truck alone after supper.

On one occasion there were so many wet holes I was required to go with the shooter for the day as his helper. You would wonder where the water came from when we were supposed to be working on permafrost.

Pushing explosive down holes time after time with 10-foot poles is a little boring, so what to do? He showed a way to amuse himself that I knew he had done before, because he did it so efficiently. First on the list was cutting down a good-sized spruce tree; this was done with explosives. Two or three small pieces of explosive and a blasting cap were wired to a tree with extra detonating wire. After backing up an appropriate distance, the charge was detonated. Down came the tree. Neat but not very exciting.

The shooter also had some old wooden loading poles with the connectors on each end that were worn out. The connectors were made of brass, as was the knife to cut the explosive to the proper size and the brass plate it was cut on. No sparks wanted.

This one particular day we put a charge down a hole and put three poles in after it. Then he was set to blow the charge, with the warning, "Watch the poles. If any of them go out of sight, get under the truck NOW! OK?"

"You bet," I replied. "I do not want to get stuck with one of those poles."

He laughed, "The chances of getting hit are pretty slim. I do this lots; only went under the truck a couple of times. Unless you are on the prairie it is difficult to find the poles, especially if you are under the truck and do not see where they come down. When they hit the ground, whether vertically or horizontally, they shatter."

"That's neat."

"Yeah, I suppose, but when you have done this as many times as I have to relieve the boredom, even this is routine. Get ready; I am going to touch her off."

With that there was a bang and a whoosh, as the three poles, still linked together, went straight in to the gray snow-filled sky. They did not go far before I lost sight of them in the snow and light cloud.

"Can you see them?" I said.

"No I was leaving the looking to you."

As I turned in astonishment to look at him after that remark, his head was turning skyward.

"I do not see them either. From past experience I would say they have reached terminal velocity by now and are earthbound. If they are coming straight down you have no chance of seeing them. At an angle maybe, but probably with no time to get out of the way."

He started bending over and heading for the truck saying,

" I hear one."

He was already bent over ready to get under the truck but I beat him with a prize-winning two-step, roll and belly flop onto the snow-packed seismic line that carried me under the truck drive shaft. I thought I did well.

"Nice dive" came to my ear as I stopped.

Quiet followed, then "Swisssshhhhh," and a very loud crack, very much like the whack us old-timers remember when the teacher struck the desk with the yardstick.

I started to crawl out from under the truck. I felt a hand on my shoulder and heard a "Wait."

Just as he finished there was another loud crack.

"Sounded like that one hit the truck didn't it?" I said.

"Yeah, it did. Let's go look."

We crawled out into the thickening snow, both angling for the back of the truck where the loudest noise had come from. Walking to the back of the truck, we were surprised at what we saw. Somehow the pole had come nearly straight down and hit end first on the plowed seismic line. It lay there shattered but held together by the brass ends. It had bounced up, landing flat crossways on the cutting surface the shooter used to prepare his charges. No damage to the truck.

"Come on, let's go see the other one. I think it landed on the line in front of the truck."

"I'm right behind you," he said.

Sure enough, 15 feet in front of the truck was another shattered pole, except this one was shattered and broken about in half.

The rest of the stuff we did that day was the routine of which you have already read.

This would be an appropriate place to mention the powder

magazine. The shooter was responsible for it and all the powder. By its name you would know it was the storage and transportation mode for our powder. After he and I had worked together a few times, he decided when he needed a hand with any other work and, when I was around, he would get me to help him.

On one of these occasions I noticed some of the sticks of Geo Gel appeared damp. When asked, he indicated some of the explosive components had separated, because the stuff was old or had not been turned to keep that from happening. He did not feel there need be a concern.

There is a picture of me holding onto the tongue of the powder magazine after it got tipped on its back end during a move, because of a load shift within.

Apparently not immediately explosive.

MICHELE LAKES

"It's time you saw Michele Lakes," was how the phone conversation started. It was Bud.

An ardent fisherman of some repute, he talked to me about going to Michele Lakes on previous occasions.

"You bet. When is a good time for you, your next days off?" I asked.

"That will be fine. We can check the weather first; no need to hike up there in the rain."

"OK we'll talk."

Now is the time to let you know our first attempt to go to Michele Lakes was not successful. We started off from Highway 11 west of Rocky Mountain House where Owen Creek crosses the highway near the park border. Owen Creek has two branches, and somehow we got on the west branch going towards the glacier on Mount Wilson that's just back of the Crossing Resort in Banff Park. When we realized our mistake it was too late that day to correct it and continue on to the lakes.

We did discover a small island of trees, mature Douglas fir growing in a secluded pocket, protected by a rock outcropping. Our misguided adventure had taken us behind the hoodoo-like outcroppings up the mountain behind the resort. We had traversed some difficult terrain to get where we were and did not want to go back that way, so we elected to come down from our lofty perch between the rock outcroppings. This proved very steep and interesting but doable, and in the end saved a lot of time.

Another attempt to reach the lakes had to be made.

"Next days off are in two days. Are you good to go? I checked the weather, it should be great."

"I'm good; we're just going for the day right?" I asked.

"Lots of folks go for overnight because of the distance, but I think we'll be good for a day hike. Travel light and fast."

"That's fine. This time we will make sure to go the right way where the creek forks."

"Now that's a plan. How about leaving here at 5 a.m.? We can start hiking up the creek by 7. I will pick you up," I replied.

"OK, see you then."

The idea was I would check anglers at the lakes and Bud would fish. He had not been there before and was itching to catch a golden trout. He was waiting at the door when I got to his house.

"Hi. Let's go. It looks like a fine day we have no time to lose."

With that we were off on another adventure. Arriving at Owen Creek, we parked the truck in the ditch, got out our gear and started walking up Owen Creek. Walking the creek was difficult because of the boulders in and along the creek bed. We found easier walking on the west side, a little way into the bush. When we came to the fork in the creek we followed the right fork that would take us to a low pass allowing us to drop down to Michele Lakes.

The last part of Owen Creek is difficult walking because the creek is in a narrow canyon and there are a numerous dry riverlets eroding each bank, so you must pick a side above these and do your best. We finally made it to the tree line where the creek commenced. From there it was over the top and down the other side to the lakes.

Approaching the height of land indicating the termination of our upward journey, there was a dip in the ground. As the whole dip became visible it looked like some farm implement had dug up the whole thing. Who knows it could be. Our trail had taken us temporarily into the federal park. From past experience we knew what it was. Bears, most likely grizzly, had been digging for hedysarum roots, one of their favorites. There was no sign of any bears. That is good; there is no place to hide or run to above the tree line. Further examination of the digging revealed it was very fresh and about half an acre in size. It was a hot summer morning with a light breeze and some of the digging was still very damp compared to the rest.

"Real fresh. You know I am not a big fan of bears; at least there are none here now," was Bud's comment.

"Yeah, that is good. The up-side is there is no other way back to the truck. We're almost breaking over the top on the way down to the lakes. When we come back we will know where this spot is. Make lots of noise and hope the wind is from our backs, so if there are any bears they will smell us and leave. How's that?"

"Like we have a choice. There is only problem: it's a plan made by government."

We both laughed. I figured with the amount of sweating we were doing with any luck we would smell worse than the bears and that would discourage them!

Over the top, we could finally see the lakes. There was a tent set up between the two lakes. We could see some people at the tent and on the shore of the upper lake.

Arriving at the tent I introduced my self as the Fish and Wildlife officer, as if my uniform shirt had not done that already. I do not usually check anglers unless they are fishing; because they do not have to show you their license unless they are fishing or you have seen them fish or are in possession of fish. It turned out they were all fishermen and only to glad to show their licenses. Their feeling was getting checked made it all worthwhile. Theirs was a four-day stay. Driving from Sylvan Lake to the David Thompson Resort, they chartered a helicopter to the lake. Two days were left on their trip. Fishing had not been that good according to them, but yes they had all caught some fish and put them back. Most of the fish had been caught in the upper lake and some in the lower. I said thanks and left to check the rest of their group.

From their tent you could see all the lower lake and some of the upper lake. I could see Bud at the lower lake casting. Two casts and he had a fish. I found the rest of the fishermen and checked them. Every thing was in order. By now Bud had moved to the upper lake. I wanted to see the outlet from the lower lake. It is supposed to be a falls in the neighborhood of 1000 feet. Arriving there and looking down I think that is right. The amount of water running out of the lakes and over the falls at that time was very little. You could take a regular step and be across the creek. It was narrow enough for me to comfortably have one foot on each side and look over the falls watching the river water turn to a spray, taking on the colors of the rainbow.

Now wouldn't that make a neat picture? I stepped to one side, got out my camera, straddled the creek once again and looked down. You bet that will make a dandy picture. I put the camera up to my eye and tried to focus on the falls. I finally got it. There was a problem: the image in the camera viewfinder kept ever so slightly swaying. What is wrong with this thing? I took the picture then realized my internal balancer was giving me a message that it did not like where I had put it and to get it out of there or something I might not like, like falling over the falls, could happen. I stepped back and took another look with both feet on one side. No swaying this time. Because I have to know why things happen the way they do I straddled the falls again and looked down without the camera to my eye. Steady as a rock. Interesting.

I looked around and there was Bud fishing his way along the shore towards me. Meeting him, I asked how he had done.

"OK I think. I was watching those other guys; they did not get as many as I did but I think they are using different bait.

"There is no one around. Let me take a cast with your rod and see if I can get one."

Handing me his rod he said, "If you get a fish it will be the unluckiest fish here."

"I know but I want to try."

Third cast the unluckiest fish was caught.

"I do not believe it; let's get a picture."

A picture was taken, the fish released; we started for the trail home. The fishermen who were staying gave us a wave as we went by. Part way up the slope we had a talk about the bear sign as we walked.

"So what kind of ideas do you have about the bear sign?" Bud asked.

"Well I don't like going through there any more than you, but if we go to either side far enough to make a difference we will be in that scrubby bush. Who knows what you might surprise in there? I vote for lots of noise when we get close. The wind is behind us so there will be no surprises for the bear or bears if there are any there. Besides, you and I both know if the bears set out to ambush us we are in huge trouble."

"This may be the final chance to see which one of us can really run the fastest."

We both laughed and continued on.

"It should be just over this hump. The wind is still at our backs; if there are bears there they would have smelled us by now," I said.

"Let's make some noise anyway."

"Whatever you like," I replied.

With that we commenced to do our renditions of *Lily the Pink* and some other unmemorable ditties from the late 50s and early 60s.

When we came in view of the bear-digging, no one was home. Even though dallying was not a good idea, I had to see how fresh the digging was. Some was real fresh. It could not have remained damp as it was for long with the 80 F day and wind.

Off we went. Going down is always good as long as you have cut your toenails so you don't bruise your nails and lose them. I am not sure of the time to get in and out, but 3 hours in and 2 to 2 1/2 out seem right.

It was a fine day and a good time had by all — even the fish I think.

MIDNIGHT TRAIL RIDE

There will always be a certain air of mystery attached to those who are fortunate enough to ride the high country. A sightseeing tourist, an outfitter and his clients, a government-paid patrol rider or you and your neighbors. Those who weren't there want to hear the whole story. You will be asked for descriptions of the legendary trails, uncompromised scenery, wildlife seen and what ever else went on.

When you have the opportunity to ride mountain trails on an experienced, trail-wise mountain horse, your experience will be unprecedented. The horse will know if there is anything in the bush within eyesight or smelling distance of the trail. It will alert you by looking, ears alert toward where it perceives some different movement, smell or sound. It is a good idea to watch the horse's behavior, as they do not miss much near or far.

The experienced ones will know how much room it takes for them to get between trees or rocks with pack boxes or a rider. Height perception is also an attribute not lost on the horse. If you come to an overhanging tree that will let the horse under without contact that is fine. What is finer? If the horse knows everything will not fit under the overhang with you in the saddle, and stops so you do not get knocked out of the saddle while you are admiring the flora and fauna. Now that's a good horse.

There are fine examples of non-bush-smart horses and their owners along most mountain pack trails. They take the form of smashed pack boxes, and usually some of their contents left by the trail. Trees with bark scraped off at pack box height may be another clue. A good horse in the mountains is like another set of eyes and ears as long as you pay attention to it.

Our horse patrols started at various locations. We always had a saddle horse and one packhorse each when traveling between patrol cabins. The patrol cabins were always stocked with food. Horse feed was supplied as needed. Day rides the packhorses got a rest.

One memorable ride started from Humming Bird Staging area followed the South Ram Trail up stream on the Ram towards Banff Park.

Two saddle horses and two packhorses were saddled, packed and ready to go. It took the rest of the day get to the cabin. On our way we passed where Ranger Creek runs into the Ram and an old trapper's cabin on the south side of the Ram. There were a number of guide camps where American hunters had gone for the day looking for elk with their guides. No action there. We passed the Head Waters Trail where it takes off for Ranger Creek and the Clearwater River. Continuing on, our hunter checking was nil but we did find lots of camps on the flats on the south side of the Ram just before the new South Ram Forestry Patrol Cabin. This cabin was built to take the place of the historical Headwaters Cabin farther up stream.

Arriving at the cabin late in the day, we unpacked, looked after the horses, ate and settled in for the night. Next morning we were up bright and early, ready for a ride down the Whiterabbit Trail. We could ride straight west of the patrol cabin and hit the Whiterabbit Trail instead of going by the historical cabin, a longer route. Our trail went up a gap between two small mountains, past two small-unnamed lakes, down to the Whiterabbit Trail. The drop down to Whiterabbit Trail was very steep — steep enough we walked the horses. The Whiterabbit Trail was well used mostly by riders who went the regular way instead of the shortcut we had used.

Our main purpose for this patrol was to check on some new guides to this particular area and let them know that we were around and did do horse patrols. We arrived at the Guide camp, situated some distance down the trail towards the North Saskatchewan River, just prior to lunch. The hunters and guides were returning from a sheep-scouting trip on some impressive sheep slopes we had seen south of their camp.

Introductions all around, then we started with the questions. We checked the hunters for licenses even though they weren't technically hunting at that moment. They were glad to oblige.

"So what did you see?" asked my partner.

"There's sheep up there but we did not see any big rams. On the ridge to the east of the trail we saw a grizzly bear rooting around."

"That's all?" I asked, sure they had seen more.

The other guide chimed in with, "There were some to the west as well but no big rams there either."

I looked at my partner and we agreed no more was to be accomplished here.

"Nice to have met you all; we will be on our way. Probably be back this way in a couple of days."

We mounted up and headed back up the trail. After a couple of creek crossings we stopped for lunch with a view of potential sheep slopes.

"So what did you think of that?" my partner said.

"Well it was about the same as most responses. You don't expect to hear all about what they saw; they don't know we won't tell our friends where guides told us there were large rams. I bet you noticed the hunters never said a word except when asked for their licenses."

"I noticed. Lots of times they are pretty quiet but some are talkative to their own demise," my partner replied.

"It makes my day when that happens," I said taking another bite of sandwich. We both laughed.

"Did you see the guide's face when I asked him which way he got to his camp, across the Saskatchewan or up the Ram?" I said.

"It was a good question, even though he looked surprised. The quickest way is across the Saskatchewan like the other guides used to do, but it looks like these guys do not like the danger of high water and a big river." My partner was right.

We took the long way back to our cabin via the Historical Ram Patrol Cabin to see if there were any occupants. There was a quad parked in front of the cabin but we could not find any one. Whoever it was must have been out scouting for sheep. We left a card saying we would be back and left for our cabin. We'd be passing there tomorrow anyway and do another check

Next day was going to be a big one. We got as much ready for the next day as we could and called it a day.

Sunrise saw us on the trail that would eventually take us to Indianhead House, a Banff Park patrol cabin. Going through the park was the shortest way to our next destination and the most hunters. We rode to the old Headwaters Patrol Cabin. Someone had been there since we left the card, but was gone again. We continued up the pack trail past some guide camps to the park boundary. One of the guides had a camp about half a mile from where the pack trail goes over a pass into the park. The camp was deserted. Everyone must have been gone hunting.

Over the pass we followed the trail on its ever-downward grade to the Parks Camp on the trail opposite a high pass to Ranger Creek. Sheep pass back and forth from the park to the province regularly through there. From this camp the Park Rangers can see any sheep or hunter activity from their tent. They have caught a few hunters trying to get sheep on their side of the line, making it worthwhile.

An electric fence around the tent and corral to keep the bears out shows parks at least practice what they preach. It would appear the camp itself is a deterrent to poachers. It can easily be seen from where hunter and sheep activity would take place. Probably it is just to let people know there is a presence there.

After our look around we carried on down the trail towards Indian Head House. Much to our surprise, a couple of hundred yards down the trail we discovered a barrel trapped in the bush on the downhill side of the trail. We determined it was a barrel full of oats. A bear had attempted theft and illegal entry. Amazingly it had not been successful. There were claw and tooth marks on the barrel attesting to the ferocity of the attack.

On to Indian Head House. It was a regular house with all the amenities: central heating, running water, an inside bathroom. When it was built, thought was given to stationing a Ranger their full time. As far as I know that did not happen.

It had a set of corrals, tack shed and some other buildings, all set up for horse patrol work. Two Rangers were supposed to meet us there that night. They showed up just as we finished supper. We talked about what we saw on the trail, which for all of us had not been much that day. Without fear of prejudice we continued the evening solving provincial and federal problems. I always wondered how ordinary folks could do that in an evening and the high-priced help never gets it done.

I should mention the parks horses did not like our horses in their corral. Upon arrival we hobbled our horses. When the parks horses showed up there was a bit of a turf war between the two groups. Each group's dominant horse did most of the kicking and neighing. The hobbles restricted ours severely.

Next morning we set out, one parks person one Fish and Wildlife person. My partner and I rode the Clearwater Trail back to its junction with the Headwaters Trail then north on the Headwaters Trail almost over to Ranger Creek and saw no one. The others on Peters Creek Trail, Condor Creek over to Forbidden Creek Trail found some hunters but no violations. Expensive day for the taxpayers.

All the horses were corralled the same as the day before, this time no hobbles. We were sitting down for supper with a fine view of the corral. Much neighing, snorting and hoof-stamping got our attention. The turf war was on again. Our side was not handicapped by hobbles this time. It appeared to me and the others in attendance that injury to one or both horses was imminent. Surprisingly there was no rush for the door to go and stop the fight, just lots of watching out the window. The flat land horse, our horse, won no contest. Somehow after the first few kicks the parks horse knew it was out-classed and walked away.

Next day we were off to Forty Mile Cabin with some stops on the way. My partner had seen something he wanted to look at on our way to Forty Mile. We got just out of the park to where the Peters Creek trail goes south towards Forbidden Creek Trail and crosses the Clearwater River. Just past there is a little hill on the trail. Near the top of the hill Mike said.

"We took a little ride down here yesterday and saw some fresh horse tracks on an old trail. I thought we should go look."

"Good idea. I haven't been this way before."

He found the trail. It left our trail and went into the bush. Not a lot of sign of use — who knows where it might lead? Going into some heavy bush and down a slight grade, it came to a creek crossing. To our surprise, where the trail crossed the creek was a barbwire fence with a farm gate. The fence extended on each side of the gate into the bush. There had to be some horses pastured here somewhere, but why fence the bush? The fence was not situated to keep the horses in when they drank. Opening the gate we went through and closed it. Our trail took a turn to the right and shortly we were in a natural pasture, the trail diminishing to almost nothing.

Continuing on, eyes open for anything, we were finally rewarded: there on our right, barely visible through the trees at the edge of the pasture, was the corner of a tent. As we approached the tent you could tell a hunting camp had been set up on the site. Whether it had been set up so it would be hard to find or see is speculative, but that could be the conclusion.

At our leisure we took a look around, admiring the setting: water handy for horses and people, what appeared to be more than ample pasture for a number of horses. Most important, there was a slight rise in the ground where the tent was pitched. The camp was not long deserted.

"I wonder who set this up?" I asked.

"Someone will know, probably the guys at the next camp. I haven't been in here before," answered Mike.

"I hope someone at the next camp knows who's this is.

Where we started off the main trail to come in here, you were first. What did you see for tracks?"

"Not much. There was solid rock on the side of the trail. I noticed marks on the rock from horseshoes. It looked like you could ride around the rock. I wondered why anyone rode over it; thought it was worth a look."

"I guess we know now why whoever it was rode over the rock: so there would not be an obvious trail off the main trail. That is how I see it," I said.

"Sounds good to me. We can look on the way out."

Compounding the use of the gate and fence were picket pins at various places where the horses had obviously been pastured. In our ride around we had not seen the fence come out of the bush along the creek anywhere.

With that we mounted up. Arriving at the gate Mike dismounted to open it. I was looking around to see where and what the fence was supposed to do from a whole new perspective. Following it upstream I saw something I could not identify.

"Mike, take a look up stream on the south side and tell me what that is." He moved around a little so he could see up the creek.

"Looks like a piece of canvas."

I urged the horse ahead half a step.

"It's the corner of the tent. Looks like the front corner."

Mike had backed up a bit to get a better view. Looking up the creek and moving around a little in the limited space allowed by the bush and trees along the creek, we were able to determine the gate had been strategically placed so dismounting to open it would, depending on weather conditions, create enough noise to alert anyone near or in the tent that someone was coming.

Very interesting. Why? We had had a good look around and not discovered anything that looked out of place, but you never know.

A person who went to all the trouble of riding off the trail at an inconspicuous place put up a fence and gate to make anyone on the trail dismount so he could see them when he was in camp would undoubtedly notice someone had been to the camp in his absence but not who!

On down the trail we went to the first guide camp. It was situated on a south-facing slope, backed into the edge of the trees with a view of the flats. A visit found the cook alone in camp. Hospitality afforded by the guides and outfitter and their staff was always supreme. We chatted about hunters, what success had been attained to this point by them, and how long they would be there.

There was always coffee, fresh buns or bread, sometimes cookies and pie — none of it store-bought. A number of camps had professional chefs. Well-fed clients are happy clients.

We continued on across the flat. There was a wagon trail here, so we could talk as we rode. "Mike do you remember the time you and I and the Parks Officer went up Peter's Creek by the park border over to Condor Creek and down Forbidden to Forty Mile Cabin? I think the parks guy went with us to the sheep camps, then back to Indian Head House."

"Yes I do but I do not remember if it was a parks guy or not,"

" I thought it was. Anyway we were both there. I remember stopping for lunch on a nice sunny knoll, some distance off the trail but so we could still see it."

"Yeah," said Mike. "But remember the guy we could not see well enough to recognize came along, and saw us eating lunch and kept on going down the trail to the sheep hunters' camps we were going to?"

"Yes and we talked about him figuring out who we were and letting everyone know. Remember, he did just that? We got there to check, found the camps, some occupied, some where their hunters were scouting. Seems to me someone told us a young deer had been shot for camp meat but that person had left camp."

"I remember something about that. We looked all over the place for any sign of the kill. We looked back of the camps in the bush to see if any meat was hanging. Never found a thing. Never located the supposed hunter either, best I can remember," said Mike.

We passed a couple of empty camps. We always rode into the camps, even if we did not see anyone, just to look around and determine when the latest activity took place. We passed a trail over to the Clearwater where a guy who looked like Yosemite Sam had a camp. Seemed there was trouble with one of the government agencies and some of his buildings were flown out by helicopter.

Our next stop was a camp right on the Clearwater River. The fellow who ran the guiding and outfitting also had a trap line there. He had a really nice trapper's cabin where his guide camp was but was not allowed to use it in conjunction with his guiding and outfitting operation. That was done out of tents

He was there; most importantly his cooks were there. Guides and hunters had gone for the day. Now it was late afternoon. Potatoes were being peeled; supper would be ready when guides and hunters returned. We were invited to stay for supper, as they often had supper twice: once for the camp crew and again when the hunters and guides returned.

We decided to wait and have supper there. We did not do too badly for ourselves but this was better. Steak, potatoes, vegetables, fresh apple pie accompanied by many tall tales of the legendary past and present.

A guide and some of the hunters showed up. A trophy elk had been shot. They had returned for a packhorse and some help. Our supper finished and offers of help turned down, we said thanks for supper, mounted up and were on our way. It was dark already. We came to the camp at the Rails. Strangely there was no one there. It was usually occupied. As we went down the bank on the Clearwater into the river crossing, Mike, who very seldom asks the horses to do more than walk, was galloping.

This was neat. I had been admiring the full moon and how it changes everything as we rode. Every thing was all black and white. Perspective was lost. He was riding his horse at a gallop on an angle into the river in front of me, and I could see him and both the horses. They were now a black and silver-gray blur riding on a silver river, spraying sheets of water in the air as they galloped for the far bank. It looked way too neat; I had to do it.

We trotted on to the cabin. The horses were watered, fed and corralled. Forty Mile Cabin one more time. We lit the stove and lantern and got ready for bed. The light was not out long and the rays of the full moon were streaming in the two windows. I listened to my cigarette box-sized radio for a while. American late night talk shows; not good.

Looking at the moon shining in reminded me of another night we were there. There were only two bunks and there were three of us. Bunk rights usually go to the person who arrives first for choice, and retention if anyone else shows up and wants to stay the night.

Our cabin partner for that night was a Forestry Patrol Officer whose summer duty was ensuring a lot of things, one being seen, flying the company flag. Make no mistake, he wrote tickets when the circumstances warranted it. He insisted we take the bunks. He had an air mattress and would sleep on the floor. We tried to convince him otherwise. He would have none of it.

It was not a bright moonlit night when we quit talking and went to bed you could see the stars very well. At 3 a.m. or so I was listening to my radio, enjoying watching the stars. Off to my left there was a thump followed by mumbled threats. The starlight from the window I had been looking out disappeared. It was our host causing the commotion. He appeared to be in a life-and-death struggle with his sleeping bag. It ended as quickly as it started. He lay back down never uttering a word.

"What the hell was that about?" I asked.

"Mouse ran over my face."

That was it; no more comments from him then or later.

Next morning we were saddling up when a wagon showed up. Yes, a real covered wagon. They look a lot like the ones you see in the western movies, usually pulled by a two- or four-horse team, maybe mules. A lot of the guides and outfitters use them to haul in their clients and equipment. Folks who just want to spend their holidays doing some trail riding use them as headquarters and take day rides. Usually there will be a tent or two set up for private sleeping accommodation. This was a popular spot, within walking distance of the Forestry outhouse. You may think that is a joke. Not true — I have been at that cabin and watched people on more than one occasion get out of their wagon, paper in hand (not the morning news) and use the facilities. One thing about it, they always looked satisfied when they left. Newspapers don't always do that.

We thanked our host for the use of the beds and left. Going over and talking to the people in the wagon we discovered they were trail riders, there for a week. Guess what? They asked about using the outhouse. Any time was the answer, just don't slam the door.

On our ride to the truck and trailer that had been moved to the Cutoff Creek Staging area we had some more time to talk about other trips.

Near the headwaters of the South Ram River there are some interesting Mountain Sheep hunting places that were very popular. Regular patrols to the area ensured, as far as we could tell, violations were kept to a minimum. On one of those regular patrols flying the flag we found ourselves in an interesting position.

Having been on the trail for a while, we stopped for a snack just on the edge of the trees so we would be difficult to see but we could see a number of popular hunting places. As we glassed, my partner noticed a pack train coming out of a little valley above the tree line. With the horses tied back in the trees and us in shadow, we stayed where we were sure we would not be seen. No sheep heads could be seen tied on the pack horses.

At a couple of miles away we could not see everything, but we got an idea what they had. In order to back up our observations we needed to stop these hunters and check them — make their licenses worth buying.

To make this happen, some planning had to take place. A decision was made to leave the horses, even though there was a chance they might whinny and give us away. The wind was right and they would not be able to see the other horses. Next time the hunters went behind a rise we moved to our chosen position.

We were on a down slope on the south side of the trail, with large pine trees and some brushy ground cover. One of these bushes was exactly where we needed it for both of us to get behind. Considering the terrain and how far away they were, we knew it would be a while before they got to us.

"We have to make sure the lead horse sees us before we get out of cover," my partner said.

"You bet. I'm ready."

We got into position so the horse coming around the tree would see us before the rider did. Love those long necks. Waiting, we watched and listened. Peering through the leaves we could see the lead horse. Now it was very close. It got to the chosen tree and immediately started looking at us, but never missed a beat, just looked. Time to move.

We both stood up less than 10 feet from the horse.

"Good afternoon. Fish and Wildlife. How was hunting?" asked Mike.

"Whoa," the lead rider yanked back on the reins, causing the horse to rear up.

"What are you doing? I didn't even see you!"

"We are waiting for the hunters to come off the mountain so we can check them. You are the first."

Turned out these folks were all in order as far as we were concerned. They'd been out for a week and not seen any sheep that were satisfactory. Home was there destination.

Anyone who has been on a wilderness horseback ride will understand there is no greater opportunity to remember other previous similar experiences.

Continuing the ride back to the truck, part of another horse patrol came to mind. We were coming down the Forbidden Creek Trail towards Forty Mile, on the flats nearing the cabin in some real heavy willow. For some reason we stopped. Just when we were ready to get going we heard what sounded like a horseshoe on a rock. Looking at each other, somehow we knew the drill: sitting and waiting, no moving, no talking.

Whoever or whatever it was could not get by us in the tangle of willows. A corner in the trail about 2 horse-lengths ahead assured surprise. We sat for what seemed like a long time. Not another sound did we hear.

Then something brown and gray came towards us at a fast trot, sniffing. A dog materialized, took one look at our horses and us and kept right on going. We looked at each other, knowing dogs do not make the kind of noise we had heard, so we sat.

Wind direction changed. There it was: the unmistakable sound of horse's hooves on rock and gravel mixed with the indistinguishable sound of human voices.

When the lead rider came around the corner, for some reason he was looking back. He turned to look up the trail when his horse stopped. His look of surprise could not be topped. His first early warning system, the dog, had failed him by not barking when strangers were on the trail. His saddle horse, which undoubtedly knew other people and horses were close at hand, had not whinnied.

The direction he was coming from indicated he was going to his camp but a check would take place anyway. In the tight confines of the willow everything was found to be in order. Turned out this trip was to take in the remainder of his sheep-hunting camp.

While we checked him and his partner and their horses, I was close enough to them to hear the lead rider say, in a highly irritated tone, "What the hell is wrong with that dog of yours?

You told me he would raise cane if there was anyone else on the trail. You know these guys are going to tell everyone how they surprised us. There is nothing worse to get around about you than having the Game Wardens surprise you."

In his defense the other rider countered with,

"You were the one who rode your horse nose-to-nose with theirs before you saw them. Your horse stopped before you knew they were there. Not only that, you were looking back when the horse stopped. Leave my dog out of this."

Our parting comments were the usual polite talk with a bit of added information that might work to encourage honesty or heighten stealth.

"We'll be here for about a month, probably get by your sheep camp again pretty soon."

Considering horse patrols at that time were most uncommon and their duration unknown, consternation and confusion were our aim. I thought we did well. My partner later informed me our latest subject was high on the illegal activity list but had as yet not been caught.

Finally we got to the truck. Gear loaded, horses loaded, we were on the way home.

"I was trying to remember some of the interesting things that happened on other horse patrols," I said to Mike.

"What about the pack rat?"

"Help me with that."

"I can't believe you don't remember that. This is what I remember. For a couple of nights a pack rat had been coming in waking us up. Traps were set but did not work. Somehow they got sprung or did not work properly. Three a.m. and there it was, fat and sassy, squatted on top of the stove eating crackers. I had no idea they were that noisy — the crackers not the pack rat."

"OK, OK. I remembered when you got to the part about the traps not working. Don't stop; let's hear your version," I said.

Looking a little miffed, Mike continued.

"Plug your ears; I am going to put a stop to this right now. You know the rest."

"Yeah, even with my ears plugged the reverberation from the shot shook the bunk and vibrated my bones. Up-side: no more cracker-crunching noises."

"That sounds about right. How long did it take for your ears to stop ringing?"

"What did you say? I can't hear so good."

Would you believe it? He even cupped his hand over his ear.

"Yeah! Yeah! I know you can hear just fine. There's a rumor going around you can hear a fly fart at half a mile."

He just looked at me and grinned and said, "Were you with me when we saw the wolves on the gravel bar?"

"No I don't think so. I have seen wolves here but not when you and I were together. Let's hear about it."

"We were coming from South Ram Cabin down the Ram. It was a really bad day. We were wearing all the clothes we had. Starting off there was 6 or 8 inches of snow, and it just kept coming. You couldn't see 2 horse-lengths ahead. You know where you come down from the old cabin and ride in the river?"

"Yeah I know where that is."

"Well not long after you get into the river, there are some little gravel islands the trail goes across. I was squinting to see through the snow without much luck, letting the horse pick its way. I could see across a little open water where the trail goes on to another gravel island. On this island eight or ten mounds of snow were spread around about the size of a big washtub. I didn't think much about it; must be driftwood or something. The horses just kept following the trail that went between the snow mounds.

We'd passed about half of them some on each side when one in front and to the side rose up and shook. It was a full-grown wolf. All the snow mounds got up in turn and turned into wolves, duly shaking themselves, stretching and yawning. While they were shaking and stretching they looked at us with little concern. No people or horses were moving. Upon completing their inspection the wolves headed off across the island into the river, crossing it, climbing the bank and disappearing into the spruce."

"That's real neat. The horses must have known what they were before they got up."

"We'll never know. I was waiting for a rodeo to start after the first one stood up but it did not happen, so you're probably right."

"It's nice people sit at home and read books, but someone has to go out and do stuff you can write about," I said.

We were talked out.

RARING TO GO

My foot was finally healed enough to work seismic again. This time the destination was the answer to one of my dreams, to go north of the Arctic Circle, 66 degrees north on your map. I do not remember the exact date in November I boarded a plane in Calgary for Edmonton with some other seismic hands. There we got on a Pacific Western DC-3 with two gas-powered radial engines, seating from 21 to 28 passengers, attaining a top speed of about 192 miles per hour for a flight to Norman Wells, Northwest Territories. I will never know how many passengers the plane may have held because the seats had been removed from one side of the plane where cargo was now tied down. I suspect that's not allowed now, combining passengers and cargo in the same space.

Norman Wells is on the Mackenzie River in the Northwest Territories of Canada, where oil seeped out of the riverbanks. It was the start of the Canol Pipeline, short for Canadian Oil, running to Whitehorse. Just in case you care, it was constructed by the US Corps of Army Engineers between 1942 and 1944. Spurs were built to Fairbanks, Watson Lake, Skagway and Haines. A Japanese threat to Alaska, which did not materialize, was a significant cause behind this huge effort. In 1947 the flow of oil was turned off. The pipeline has not been used since 1947. The road beside the abandoned pipeline is kept in various states of repair but is mainly used by hikers.

We landed at Norman Wells. During the previous summer the seismic company shipped by barge from Hay River on Great Slave Lake up the Mackenzie River all the equipment required to run the seismic program for the winter except food. Cats, trucks, fuel, dynamite blasting caps, powder magazine, bunk and eating trailers, power plant, propane, sleds. (No, not the sleds we have now; ones that haul many tons and are pulled by cats.) The food was flown in once or twice a week. There was enough lumber to build a most essential item: an outhouse. There will be a story later about the legendary outhouse.

As it turned out we had to wait at Little Chicago for about a week, because the ground was not frozen hard enough for the cats to make a road to our designated site and start the seismic program. A few words about Little Chicago. It is just north of 67 degrees, inside the Arctic Circle on the right bank of the Mackenzie River. Used as a native camping place for eons, it was not called Little Chicago. The site has a historical connection to the Klondike Gold Rush. Some prospectors from Chicago stopped there to hunt and trap to make money so they could continue their journey to the Klondike. Hence Little Chicago. Looks like a tough way to get to the Klondike at any rate. In a straight line it is halfway between Fort Good Hope and Inuvik. It now has a native name.

While we were waiting for the ground to freeze, we checked equipment and built the outhouse. It was quite an outhouse, constructed by yours truly and one other. There was limited plywood, 2 x 4s and nails. Those are all the details you need. It was a single-holer, built ultra-strong on direction from the boss. Ultra-strong was required because of the amount of times we would have to move it, plus the ever-present danger it might fall off the truck during a move. It did fall off during a move; the door got wrecked and was repaired.

A few nights of -40 F with daytime temperatures of -30 F soon fixed the ground frost. The smaller cats cleared the foot and a half or 2 feet of snow off the forest floor, the frost went down and the big D8 and D9 cats could then build our road. Finally we were on the road to somewhere.

We were each assigned trucks to drive. The trucks were mid-50s Ford 1- tons that saw previous seismic experience farther south. They came here to terminate their service and turn to rust. Considering this all took place in the late- to mid-50s, they should be well on their way by this writing. The trucks were equipped with the latest innovation to help keep you from getting stuck: non-slip rear ends. That means when the rear wheel on one side spins, the one on the other side mechanically locks up so neither will spin independently. That is fine as long as you want to go straight. When you are on a frozen, snow-covered seismic line where every corner is right-angled, your truck is loaded, and you have 2 tons of trailer pushing you straight, turning becomes nearly impossible. You might have to take two or three tries to get lined up so you can get around a corner.

The other issue with the trucks was the heaters. Traveling along at 10 or 20 miles an hour due to the roughness of the cutline, the heaters still would not keep the truck cabs warm. It was not long before the operators installed more heaters. The shooter, a German fellow, installed five heaters — that's right, five. They were in every conceivable place you could imagine. When it was 50 below it still was not enough. I am getting ahead of myself.

Our first day on the road to our semi-permanent camp was

interesting. The cats had done the best they could to make the line smooth. It did not work. After a long slow day's travel, we arrived at our first semi-permanent campsite with our accommodation in tow. The word "day" is relevant only in hours. There was zero direct sunlight. It was light enough to work outside and see from 10 a.m. to 2 p.m. No sun had been seen since we arrived and was not expected back till some time in February. There was a predestined order for the trailers and trucks to park on the cleared area, prepared by the cats prior to their moving on to create more seismic line.

Please remember we are talking late 50s, when seismic camps were a camp, not a fully enclosed, roofed area with cook, recreation trailers and office washroom facilities all heated as one. Each trailer had its own diesel furnace and circulation fan. You will find out what happens when the fans quit. Not nice.

Our camp was set up with the power plant in the centre, cords going every direction. One side had plug-ins for trucks; from the other side cords ran to trailers. We could not afford to let the trucks run all night. Down south where there was fuel delivery to the camps, that was common.

More trial and tribulations to come.

BROKEN GRADER

Any of you who have traveled on winter roads built on muskeg know they get very rough in a big hurry. Making and finishing a cutline with a D-6 Caterpillar(Bulldozer) is fine. They leave it smooth enough for trucks to pass over a few times without getting too holey (well maybe on Sundays). After that they need maintenance with a grader.

I believe the thinking behind the maintenance was less truck repairs. With trees, humps and snow removed and flattened out, you could drive a vehicle as small as a two-wheel drive, half-ton truck on them. Speaking of half-tons, the seismic crew had one Chevy half-ton with torsion bar suspension everyone liked to ride in, because it gave the smoothest ride even when the line was rough. It was interesting watching this truck approach and see the torsion bars go up and down in a blur as they absorbed seismic line holes.

Back to road maintenance, the grader not only filled the holes with snow, which did not last long, but kept the creek and river crossings we used in shape. Approaches to lakes were somewhat more troublesome. You were going from a soft surface (snow) to a very hard one (ice). Where the two surfaces met, the snow was always getting pushed out of the way by the tires coming off the ice or trying to get on. The result, a hole big enough break something, often the truck springs, unless the driver slowed down. There is another story about truck parts breaking from not slowing down and cold weather. That's when we had real winter: -20 to -45 Fahrenheit for weeks, not the non-event it has turned into now.

I was always interested to know if the expense incurred in trucking the grader from Calgary to Hay River, by barge from Hay River up the Mackenzie River, finally to Little Chicago paid off in terms of maintenance savings on the other vehicles. That was truly the sole purpose of having the graders maintaining the roads.

One afternoon, on our way to camp for supper, we came over a rise to see the grader off in the distance stopped at a T-intersection in the cutlines, a couple of miles away. As we approached, its profile took on a strangely abnormal shape. It looked like it was leaning forward. We speculated that the front wheels must be in a hole. Maybe there was something else wrong, since no operator could be seen.

We looked in disbelief as we got closer — the grader was broke in half! How could this happen to a grader grading snow, sticks and clearing snow of lake ice? We all had to get out and have a look.

Just ahead of the cab where the front frame attached under the cab, the whole frame was cracked wide enough we could put our fingers in the crack. The crack went right through to the other side. The front portion of the machine dropped down; the cab leaned forward. Yup, broken.

I do not remember all the details how but it was fixed by putting it back to its normal profile then welding the cracks and then welding plates over the welded cracks. As I recall, it graded some more but I do not know if it went back to Calgary.

Probably would not pay its way!

FIRST BOW SHEEP

Back in the old days when the mountain sheep outnumbered their food, biologists got nervous. Some places the sheep had to browse down close to the dirt. The piles of sheep droppings at their bedding sites were copious. Truly a bad sign, but what to do? How about an archery season for ewes?

Hunting records show archery success is not high. Couple that statistic with the opportunity to limit the number of permits for a specific Wildlife Unit and you have a management tool that can reduce the sheep population back to where there is enough feed.

This was good news to me. I knew where there were lots of ewes not far from the highway, right in my favorite hiking place. I could ride a trike, a pedal bike, or a Rokon to their location.

A what? A Rokon. It's a two-wheel-drive motorcycle, sprockets and chains front and back. My friend, Wayne, happened to be a proud owner of one.

Having watched Wayne operate it, I can attest to its unbelievable capabilities. The best part: a Rokon follows game trails well, like game; you've never seen anything like it. It requires somewhere for the tires to get a grip. A capable operator will have time to drive and look for game. The only thing that slows it down is loose gravel on a very steep hill, or deep water. More about the Rokon later.

A date was set for the hunt. I was sure success was guaranteed, likely within hours, judging by past sheep sightings. Early one morning in September we were loaded and ready to go. The Rokon and my mountain bike were loaded in the back of the truck with the rest of our day's needs. The Rokon has no seating for two, and I did not have a trike. This was before quads and cell phones. My mountain bike was not as fast as the Rokon but faster than walking, and I was assured a sheep could be tied on it. Besides, I had traveled this trail before on a mountain bike.

Arriving at the trailhead, we unloaded our gear. We mounted our machinery and headed off down the trail. We stopped in some bush near where we should see sheep and started to walk. The sun was just coming up to our backs, wind in our faces, sheep just ahead. Everything looked good. Cautiously we approached the sheep bedding area to find — nothing. Absolutely nothing. We scoured the whole area: ravines, little pockets of bush — nothing. Where were they? It was time to do some serious glassing.

The early morning sun on the mountains revealed their presence. They had gone across the creek to their other favorite spot on a different mountain. There was nothing to do but to cross the creek and see if we could get close over there.

We were off, down the trail and across the creek. Not even the Rokon could manage the terrain on the other side of the creek. There was a steep bank dense with bush, and loose rock and dirt on side slopes with more dense bush. It would have stopped the Rokon. It was bad enough for people. We could even see where the odd elk had spun out. However, past these obstacles we saw the sheep.

Finally having battled our way to a place where binoculars

could be used to look for the sheep, we were presented with another challenge. The sheep had moved up the mountain to what to them must have been better grazing or bedding. I had walked over those beds on previous occasions and there was one everywhere there was a hint of a flat spot. Copious sheep droppings surrounded them. As we watched, they continued a slow but relentless feeding and walking pace to the top. We knew by the time we got there they would be gone, unless they bedded down. To get where they were, our continued observation would be interrupted by undulations in the ground and patches of bush not to mention ravines.

Gone again. Now where did they go? We found a better place to glass from. We found them, inside the White Goat Wilderness area, which was closed to hunting.

"I see another group over there," said Wayne as he pointed to the west down the slope we were sitting on.

"Yeah, I see them, but it doesn't look like as many as we saw from the other side of the creek. They must have split up somewhere."

"You've been here before. Where do you think they went?"

"There are way too many places here sheep could hide. We could walk right by them and not even know. Just to the north and east of where we are now there is another favorite bedding spot. Let's go look there," I suggested.

"Lead the way."

We headed down slope a little and then traversed, trying to stay in the trees out of sight of sheep's prying eyes, arriving shortly within sight of my goal. Just as we got in a position to glass, a sheep appeared not more than 100 yards away. Seldom do ewes travel alone, so we stayed in the trees, waiting for more action.

"There's another one coming around the rocks to the left," Wayne said.

"Yeah, and there's some to the left now too. See them?"

"I see them. OK, now that we have found them, how are we going to get close to them? There's not much cover."

"You're right. Let's wait here where they can't see us and see what they do. We have some time," I suggested.

"Sounds good," was the reply.

We settled in, basking in the sun, eating our lunch, just waiting. It took some time but the sheep finally finished grazing and settled down just as we finished our sandwiches.

You may think this was a problem; however, it was good fortune for us. With the number of undulations in the ground, and a small ravine and some bush, the topography actually made it possible for one of us to be able to get within shooting range of one sheep that was bedded on a rock promontory facing away from us. Taking another look around, we satisfied ourselves a sneak could be accomplished.

We just got started when three buck mule deer jumped up in front of us from one of the ravines ahead, going the length of it in their hopping gate.

"Remember when I told you about how big the mule deer are up here?" I whispered. "That looks like the one I saw when I was here hiking two months ago. Now he's got his buddies with him."

"I haven't seen mule deer that big since I was antelope hunting out by Oyen. These may be bigger. The only thing that's better about the Oyen deer is you can drive your truck to them."

Fortunately the sheep had not seen the deer run, so were not spooked.

The sheep was bedded on the edge of classic escape habitat.

Two steps forward and it would be on a rock wall only navigable by sheep. I could not see the sheep from our present position, but knew from past experience where it should be.

By the time we were within 50 yards of the sheep, it knew we were there, even though our sneak had been in cover, though minimal. It looked around at us but showed no signs of nervousness. It turned back the way it had been looking and appeared to be enjoying the view.

More sneaking. I was uncomfortable with shooting over 40 yards, particularly at an animal lying down and facing away from me. I went the last 10 yards on my belly, pretty much out in the open. The sheep was now paying more attention.

I got to what I thought was about 40 yards and started to get to my knees for a shooting position. This made the sheep nervous. It stood up, turned broad side and looked at me.

I was now on my knees, sighting just back of the front shoulder, and released my arrow. It flew straight off into the perfect blue mountain sky, just over the sheep's back into the "great wherever". The sheep took one step forward as the arrow passed over its back and was gone to live another day.

"Looked about 2 inches over the back," I said to Wayne as he walked up behind me.

"With any luck we will see some more before were done," he said.

"Let's go see where it would have fallen if you would have hit it. It may have been difficult to get," Wayne said.

We walked over to where the sheep had disappeared. It was vertical rock for about 400 feet straight down. There were sheep on the rock face as we looked down and on the grass below. I guessed the closest one would be the one I shot at, about 40 yards straight down.

"It's probably a good thing you didn't get that one. It would have been a job to get down there and get it out," said Wayne.

"Actually it isn't that bad. Lot's of extra walking, down around some cliff faces and back up again," I said.

We sat and watched the sheep end up on the grass below the rock face where they started grazing. As they grazed we decided there was not enough time to go down and sneak around them for another hunt. From this position we could also see the sheep pasture where I thought there should have been sheep in the morning when we were there. Guess what. They were there now. We continued to work our way back the way we had come, watching for ewes. None were found.

Back at the creek we got on the Rokon and rode across the creek. Arriving at the top of the creek bank, just north of where we had seen the sheep from the other side of the creek, we left the Rokon with my pedal bike and walked to the grazing area. At first glance, not a sheep to be seen. We moved along the main trail to the south and there, down one of the numerous, small, grass-covered ravines, were sheep.

A strategy session was held. I would go back one ravine from where the sheep were and go down it till I was parallel to the sheep. How would I know when I was parallel, you ask? Wayne would stay out of sight of the sheep but in my sight and guide me by hand signals.

No time to waste, the sun was down. Down the ravine I went, watching Wayne's signals. Now it was time for the shot.

I forgot to mention, we made a decision that from the top of one of the ravines to the top of the other was about 35 yards. I peered over the top of the first ravine. Sure enough, there they were, grazing their way down to a vertical drop off. The biggest one was standing broadside to me, just the way it should be.

I came to my knees and drew back, aiming just back of front shoulder. I released and the arrow was in flight.

"It looks high," I mourned. "Not again! Wait, no — it's right on the mark!" I was ecstatic.

The arrow struck the spine just back of the front shoulder. The shot was high. It must be the thin mountain air that makes arrows fly funny.

As you may know, when the spine is hit all motion ceases and the animal immediately goes down. In this case, this was a good thing as the drop-off was only yards away.

I walked down to the sheep and met Wayne. It was about 200 feet down the barely walkable slope from the main trail.

"Well, let's take the guts out and see if we can carry it. If not we will have to do some butchering."

"I don't think so," Wayne said confidently. "The Rokon will haul it up that sheep trail and we're on our way home."

I looked at him in the fast fading light and said, "You have to be kidding! The tires on that thing are the same size as the sheep trail; it's straight up on one side of the trail and nearly straight down on the other side, never mind how steep the trail is."

"Let's take the guts out and I'll show you what it can do."

I still was not convinced.

I yammered on about the Rokon as he walked away to get it. Back he came, navigating the trail like a sheep.

The only trouble we had with our venture was turning the machine around to face back uphill without it getting away on us. That accomplished, I followed Wayne's instructions on how to load the sheep. While I worked, Wayne also informed me about the size of white tail and mule deer it had hauled, tied on this same way.

Trussed up like a Thanksgiving turkey, the sheep was deemed secure enough to reach the top of the hill and, eventually, the truck. There could be no movement from the sheep carcass or it may cause the machine to go out of control with everything ending up hundreds of feet below.

Off the Rokon went, headlight lighting up the oncoming night and sheep trail. I stood in amazement, watching as machine and sheep gained speed, eventually cresting the hill. I wouldn't have believed it if I hadn't seen it.

"That was way too neat and saved us a lot of work. Pretty impressive."

"Practice is what does it," he replied modestly.

I rode my mountain bike back to the truck following the Rokon. Another adventure was over.

YELLOWKNIFE OR BUST

Strange things really do happen in the land of the midnight sun.

Jean, the girls and I were living in High Level, where trips to the Northwest Territories were easy from a distance-of-travel standpoint, but difficult in terms of everything else. We recognized that our proximity to a place that had such diversity would only last for a short time, so trips there seemed like a good idea.

One summer we decided to rent a tent trailer from a neighbor. We could pull it behind our car. It was nothing fancy — basically a canvas tent on a tin box with wheels and a trailer hitch. There was a fold-out table and sleeping platforms for four.

I loaded the trailer with our personal items and about a week's worth of groceries, keeping an eye on balancing the weight in the car and trailer. I wanted to ensure everything would ride properly and the back of the car would not drag bottom when we went though the soft spots and holes for which the Mackenzie Highway 35 was famous. We were just past the town limits when trouble started: we bottomed out. Two miles further it happened again.

"Jean we are going to have to rearrange our load," I said, as I pulled over while nearly being consumed by dust from a passing truck.

"We aren't that far from home; let's go home and rearrange where it is not so dusty," Jean suggested.

"That sounds like a good idea," I said, as I turned after the last cloud of dust disappeared.

Upon arrival, we rearranged our load to accommodate the weak rear car springs and not much better trailer springs.

"OK, let's go," Jean said to the girls, who were patiently waiting to get going. Apparently we did a good job, as the attacks by the soft spots and holes in the highway to the underside of the car were nearly zero after that.

"With all this new gravel, it's a good thing you put on new front mud flaps and repadded the gas tank to stop the flying gravel from puncturing it," Jean commented.

"No kidding! This part must have just been re-graveled," I replied.

We continued on through the seemingly never-ending dust. Light breezes crossways to the road — in the few places there were no trees — provided some respite. We traveled north through Meander River, the location of a Hudson's Bay store and native settlement situated on the banks of the Meander River. (What a coincidence!) Our next destination was the community of Steen River.

You will never guess where it is located: just off the Steen River on Highway 35. It boasted a privately owned store, providing very similar service to that provided at the Hudson's Bay store in Meander River 45 miles south. Both stores did very well buying fur from the local trappers and supplying their needs. Tourists were not a big item in 1968 — probably too much dust, although it may have been the bugs. We'll talk about the bugs later.

Both locations had Provincial Government Forest Ranger

Stations. The one at Steen River is the one I mention in *POACHERS BEANS & BIRCH BARK*. That's the story about the wolf eating out of the garbage barrel lit by psychedelic northern lights. Next we were on to the Northwest Territories border.

At the border there was a small log building, which was the tourist information booth. Some days it was; that day it was not. But it did let us know that we were officially "north of 60" degrees north on Highway 1 in the Northwest Territories. We had been here before, so didn't need assistance. Onward we pressed, our goal being the Alexandra and Louise waterfalls.

I have been to the Niagara Falls and the Victoria Falls in Africa and, for my money, these falls are equally as impressive. While they may be not as big, there are a lot less tourists and the accompanying trappings. Wilderness is to my liking.

"Look you guys! Tourists!" I exclaimed.

We all stared at four people sitting around a picnic table next to a mega-sized motor home with, you guessed it, U.S. plates. You can see the falls in its entirety from their location as well as the road. We pulled up, parking just past their motor home that took up half the parking area.

"Dad, what do they have on their heads? It looks like some kind of net," said one of the girls.

I replied in a quiet voice, "Don't stare girls; they can't help it. They aren't used to the bugs." This caused an elbow in the ribs from Jean (well, I thought it was a quiet voice) who thinks they turned to look at us because of what I said. We continued on to the viewpoint for the falls, stopping to watch the tea-colored water cascade over the falls on its way to the Arctic Ocean.

On our way back to the car, we passed the tourists, said "Hi", they nodded, and we carried on to our car. As we got in the car Bonnie said, "Dad why were they trying to eat with those nets on? Mosquito bites won't kill them."

"You are right Bon, but they do not know that."

I looked at Jean and we both started to laugh. Mosquitoes had been biting Bon since she was born. She had reached the ripe old age of five with no ill effects. We carried on to Louise Falls. It is the most picturesque of the three falls. The other one is coming up. Water cascades over the top lip of the falls, descending a number of irregular rock steps of various heights and depths before reaching the swirling river below. Record-sized pike may be caught at the base of these falls. From the viewpoint, we negotiated the rather precarious trail with Susan, aged two, on my back. The view of the falls from the river was truly worth the effort. (Sorry, no picture.)

Back down the highway to Enterprise. Not much there but a service station and highway junction: Highway 1 to Yellowknife or Highway 2 to Hay River, where you find junctions to Highways 5 and 6. We continued on, following Highway 1 as our final destination was Yellowknife.

As we drove, we reminisced about what was, to us, an astounding coincidence. One of the other times we came to the N.W.T. we had stopped at Paradise Gardens, which was situated between the Northwest Territories border and Hay River. What drew our attention was the sign on the highway advertising fresh vegetables. We wanted to see how successful a garden was this far north. Sure enough, right along the banks of the Hay River was a garden plot sporting all your common garden vegetables. After getting out of the car, we saw someone coming towards us from the house.

"Good afternoon; how are you folks?" came the cordial greeting.

"Just fine," Jean replied. "Your garden looks very good."

When I heard the voice I turned to look and listen. I could not believe it.

"What the hell are you doing way up here growing vegetables?"

He had not been paying any attention to me but he was now. I approached him. A hard look came from under his hat and he took another step closer.

"Well for crying out loud I haven't seen you in a long time. What brings you here?"

That's what people say when they recognize you and cannot remember your name. They're buying time. I would give him all he needed, I thought.

"We're just on a little holiday and saw your sign and wanted to see your garden. We live in High Level and wanted to compare the gardens. I had no idea it was you."

By now his wife had showed up and was listening. I did introductions all around except for his wife who introduced herself. I had remembered his name with good reason. He was the foreman for the City of Calgary when I got dust on the freshly pained house and broke all the windows with the flusher truck. (These stories are in this book.)

"Come on, let's have a look around. We just made tea; you can stay and have some."

"Sure we can," I said.

We had a look around, followed by a nice visit where we joked about old times with the City. With a final farewell and "Thanks for tea" we were off. Jean agreed the visit at Paradise Gardens was worth the stop, and suggested we go there again when we had time.

Traveling west on Highway 1 to the Mackenzie River Ferry,

we finally arrived at the Kakisa River and Kakisa River Campground. It is a relatively short river coming out of a lake to the south of the highway. We traveled here every spring from High Level to fish for Arctic grayling. Their limited run from the Mackenzie River to the face of Kakisa Falls on the south side of the highway does not stop their frantic spawning efforts, usually on May 24.

We pulled in to spend our first night on holidays at a familiar place. It all brought back old memories. On one occasion, some of the boys from High Level and I came to fish for grayling. We decided after limiting out in a big hurry that we should go take a look around. Following the highway towards the ferry, we came across a creek we could step across, which was running through a culvert under the road to the river. Its insignificant size was inconsistent with the number of vehicles parked there. We stopped to have a look.

Some of the folks already there took a look at us and our license plate and turned back to continue what they had been doing: shooting fish. Our approach did not deter them.

I still to this day wonder why someone would waste ammunition to shoot fish when the fish were so thick you could put your hand in the water and, with some patience, catch them. One scoop of a dip net would give you your limit.

Anyway, we watched for a few minutes, then left. Somehow the Fisheries people in Hay River got all the pertinent information they needed and prosecutions resulted. Another time, our family arranged a May 24 weekend holiday at the Kakisa River Campground with our neighbors. Arriving, we set up our private accommodations and had supper. After the traditional roasting of marshmallows we were off to bed. We knew it would be a little cool so we brought Arctic sleeping bags, the -50 F kind, to ward off the night chills. Enough for everyone, except for yours truly, who had to sleep in the 1955 sleeping bag from his first bear hunting trip in 1955. We were all tucked snug in our bags, the nighttime facilities close at hand in anticipation that night assistance may be required. Sure enough, the call came; mother responded as always. Mission accomplished.

Time wore on. Much stirring and squirming was happening in the bag next to me. I asked a question. "I can not get warmed up," came the frigid reply. Apropos, considering the temperature in the tent was below freezing. With his damsel in distress, what could this dutiful husband do but leap into the frigid air and then dive back into the adjacent sleeping bag, thereby rescuing said damsel? My rescue was followed by some repositioning, with the damsel ending up on the opening side of the sleeping bag, where the snaps are.

No one needs to be told how much heat is generated by a 20-something male body, no matter the circumstances. Before long, arms and head were sticking out; turning over had to be done or perish. But then the snaps popped open and, with a startled gasp, the fair damsel was unceremoniously dumped out of the steaming hot bag onto a very frosty tarp.

What happened next you may have already guessed: we ended up back in our original sleeping bags. One of us was grinning!

Oh yes, the next morning there was a thin coat of ice on the water bucket in the tent.

"What about the time you and your dad came here fishing? Why don't you tell the girls?" suggested Jean.

"Granddad and I came for a one-day fish. He and Gamma were at our house looking after you and me, while Mum was in

Edmonton having Sue," I said to Bon. "He was very keen after I told him about all the fish. When he lived in Nordegg, every spring summer and fall night were spent fishing.

"When we arrived at the base of the falls there were some other fishermen from High Level. They were just leaving for Hay River to repair a flat they got on the way to fish. I told them I had a flat too. Their immediate response was, "Give it to us; we're going anyway." In the north, you shouldn't travel with only spare, and it was taken for granted you carried two.

We got our tackle ready and went to the base of the falls. Spawning was in full swing. We could see Arctic grayling everywhere we looked. Dad, even with all his fishing experience, said he had never seen so many fish in one place. We had our waders on in case we needed to go up- or downstream, and to stand in the water to cast. We were in the water casting and I pointed to Dad's feet. There were so many grayling swimming around him that you could hardly see his feet. It was hard to catch one under 16 inches. He was impressed.

By the time our repaired tire returned we had caught our limit and were ready to go home. When we arrived home, Dad went on and on to my Mom about all the fish, while we were cleaning them. He also told her about the flat we got coming home. Needed all the spares.

After my story-telling was finished, we got on Highway 3 to the ferry. We were all watching to see who would see the sixth- or seventh-longest river in the world first. The Mckenzie is impressive in its width, being over 3 miles wide in places, and makes the Peace River look pretty small. A ride across the river takes about 20 to 30 minutes. Just on the other side is Fort Providence and the rest of the highway to Yellowknife, our destination.

On the other side of the Mackenzie there didn't seem to be as much traffic. We traveled northeast through the seemingly endless bush, rock and muskeg till we reached a sign saying "Edzo". We knew it was some sort of settlement just off the highway, so we went in for a look.

It was a short drive to what turned out to be a clearing in a small piece of spruce forest. Some modest houses of the day were being constructed. Somehow we knew Edzo was a Federal Government effort to move the Native folks to a new location from Rae, just up the road at a nearby lake. Even with our limited knowledge of insect problems in the north, we knew a settlement in a damp spruce forest was a bad choice. We carried on to Rae.

Rae was a bit farther off the highway, situated just off the north arm of Great Slave Lake. As you drive into Rae, the landscape goes from stunted trees to muskegs to exposed rock. The entire community is built on rock. Not very scenic, but when you consider for four months each year there's nothing but biting insects to hassle you 24-7, living on rock with a lake breeze is a pretty good idea. This had been the native way for centuries.

A Hudson's Bay store was present, perched on the rock as were other buildings. On an island not far off shore there were a number of sleigh dogs.

"Look at that," I said, pointing to the island covered with dogs. "It's just like the stories about the North where the community has an island they put the sleigh dogs on for the summer."

"Dad who feeds them?" one of the girls asked.

"I imagine someone goes out once a week or so with some meat, fish or moose and the dogs go to it."

Jean and I had a discussion about how interesting Rae was,

and how short-sighted the government people were to try to move an established community into a bug-infested forest. I recently learned that, in spite of sanitation and water conditions at Rae not being the best, the natives never did move to Edzo. (Guess who is living in the houses the government built. Government employees. Go figure!(Probably commuting to Yellowknife.)

We continued to look around Rae then headed back for the highway. The manager at Fox Lake Hudson's Bay store east of Fort Vermilion managed the store in Yellowknife before going to Fox Lake. While he was in Yellowknife he built a small cabin on Great Slave Lake. When he found out we were going to Yellowknife, he told us how to locate his cabin. It was on the west side of the north arm of the lake. We located the road into it and went for a look.

We found a very nice, compact cabin. We took two of the shutters off to have a look inside. All the items you would expect in a northern cabin were present. Curtains on the windows and a tablecloth were not expected. It was spotless. When we talked about the cabin, he mentioned his friends in Yellowknife were using it in his absence.

We decided to spend the night in our tent trailer near the cabin. Staying there we could use the lake access and look around some more. A small beach of fine gravel encouraged us to try a swim. There was a breeze that we weren't sure would be strong enough to keep away the dreaded horseflies, but we were hot and going to try anyway.

Water in northern lakes is always cold. This lake was freezing. We all got soaked and stood up in the chest-deep water. The horsefly assault was immediate and relentless. Suffering a few bites, we made it to our towels and safety. I haven't mentioned much about the other insects of all kinds in this story but they were there in the millions, every one hungry and looking for a piece of us. We were used to insects, being from northern Alberta, but their dispositions, numbers and crankiness seemed to have increased since we got into the Northwest Territories.

Curiosity satisfied and, as usual, well fed by Jean, we were off to bed. Being mid-July there was no real darkness this far north, but in no time we're all asleep.

I awoke to a thump. Then "thump" again. "It must be raining," I thought. "Thump, thump," then "thump" again.

"What is that?" Jean asked, now awake too.

"I don't know. I thought it was rain but we've heard rain on canvas before and it didn't sound like that."

I got up and unzipped one of the interior canvas window covers. The thumping continued. I could see blurred movements in the half-light. The thumping was coming from the horizontal and sloped canvas on the outside of our tent trailer. The thumping was also increasing in intensity and volume.

"I'll be darned; you know what it is? It's horseflies hitting the canvas; you can barely make them out. Why would they do that?"

"Well that's a first for us. I wonder if they will quit?"

"I don't know maybe if it rains."

It was all of 2 a.m. This could be a long night.

Sleep finally came amidst the incessant thumping. I woke up to bright sunshine and checked my watch: 3 a.m. Oh goodie. Well at least it was light enough to read. It finally struck me why the horseflies were attacking our tent trailer. Our hasty retreat after their attack during swimming was not enough; they wanted another piece of us.

A few hours later, we were driving into Yellowknife. The first thing we saw was the airport. Just to the left was a long narrow lake with a campground beside it; looked nice. We continued on into town. Our expectations were rewarded: office towers and multi-storey hotels. After two years of living in a community with nothing taller than four stories, coupled with a trip through the wilderness, Yellowknife was an oasis of sorts.

A drive around the city was interesting. We saw the new construction with houses having their basements blasted out of bedrock. Some folks were making a stab at gardening — in some cases, quiet successfully. Lots of flowers in boxes and other containers were on display, although not a lot of lawns.

Our drive continued to Old Yellowknife. It is predominately situated on the lakeshore. There were lots of float planes and boats, also some old buildings and shops to explore at a later time. On our way back to the only campground we had seen, we found a Barney's Kentucky Fried Chicken and a convenience store.

We pulled into the campground and found out the City ran it. You find a stall that suits you, park your rig, and it's yours. Someone came along every day from the city to check occupancy and collect money. There was a washhouse with toilet and shower for all. The best part was the sandy beach on the lake where kids were playing in the water and sand.

"How about Fried Chicken for supper?" Jean suggested. The girls agreed, saying, "Let's go now Mom."

"It's a little early, but we could go now and avoid the suppertime rush."

I was already heading for the car, and a short time later saying "Hi. We'd like two buckets of chicken please."

"Sorry, you will have to come back at about 4:30."

"Why, don't you have chicken ready now?"

"It comes on the plane from Edmonton. The plane arrives about 4:00."

I am sure my mouth dropped open. How much money can you make on fried chicken paying airfreight ? We checked the prices; they seemed to be in line with what you would pay farther south — a few bucks more, but not airfreight high.

She really made me feel good by saying, "You must be holidayers."

"Yes we are, but this is the first time I have been to one of your places and there was no chicken."

"Well it is more expensive to try and raise them here than it is to fly them in. They come from Edmonton every day. We cook the already-prepared bird."

"Thanks we'll be back."

Much discussion took place in the car about the chicken as we drove back to the campground to wait. What an ideal waiting place, right beside the airport. Watch for the four o'clock chicken plane.

The plane arrived; we left a few minutes after and still weren't there first. When all was said and done, the chicken tasted the way that chicken always tastes.

We spent three days in Yellowknife touring around and swimming in the lake. Interestingly the lake had another use. As I mentioned, the lake was across the highway from the airport. On the second morning of our stay I looked up towards the highway along the campground access road. There was a floatplane coming right at us, not making a sound. For an instant, confusion reigned supreme in my brain. What was happening?

Then I saw a custom-made, self-propelled gantry holding

the plane suspended, so the floats would not touch the ground as it made its way across the highway. By now most of the campground residents were out to watch. Eventually the aircraft was freed from its transporter and floating on the lake. It was not long and off it went to do its work, leaving us all to wonder about its final destination.

Further exploration of Yellowknife included a trip to the gold mine that started everything. We just looked at the entrance as there were no tours. In old Yellowknife we had a look at the floatplanes. It seemed after their initial launching at the lake, they ended up here tied to a dock. Large commercial fishing boats and small private boats lined the boat dock as well.

A kind of trading post-looking store attracted our attention. We were not disappointed. On the walls, floor, and hanging from the ceiling were items a trapper could not do without. The most wise owner had seen the light; also on display were souvenirs for tourists.

That was our last day in Yellowknife. Next morning we said goodbye to our campground neighbors and headed south. Arriving at the Fort Providence Ferry crossing we had to wait. As we waited, looking upriver towards Great Slave Lake, we could see some kind of sizeable boat approaching. Our ferry was almost back when it finally got close enough to be recognizable. It was a tugboat pushing a number of loaded barges. By the time we were loaded, a look from the ferry showed two barges being pushed, one beside the tug and two behind. All were close-coupled.

We continued on, stopping in Hay River to get gas. This was in the days when all service stations served gas.

"Fill 'er up?"

"Yup."

174

I said "yup" as I was getting out of the car, and then turned to see who this person was. I could not quite believe what I saw. There were rivulets of blood running down his cheek to his jaw line and chin. I needed another look! As he put the pump nozzle in to fill the car I got a better look. Sure enough, it was blood. You could see it at the base of each sideburn heading down his jaw line.

It was an 85 F-plus day. Everyone was sweating. Black flies like nothing more than heat and sweat. Where the sweat was coming off the end of his side burns the black flies were congregating. Looked like a party.

"Black flies are bad today?"

"No kidding I have terrible trouble with them. I should get some more repellent, but it doesn't last long when you sweat," he replied matter of fact.

Enough said. I thought he must know he's bleeding.

Our final drive in Hay River was to the lakeshore to look at the landing where all the river barges and tugboats were kept in the winter. Huge squared timbers called a "slipway" were set in the lake shore, running up from the water's edge far enough to get the vessels out of harm's way from floods and ice. Slipways were usually greased prior to use so as not to be too hard on the boat. The vessel to be stored was piloted parallel to the shore, hooking cables to appropriate places on the vessel and pulling on the cables with a caterpillar till the vessel reached the desired location on the slipways.

Looking out across the lake from here was like looking out on the ocean. Now we could go home.

TRANSOM TRESPASSERS

Our return trip to Inuvik after Christmas was not near as exciting as the one from Inuvik to Edmonton before Christmas. Some one else loaded the plane and unloaded it.

We arrived in Inuvik a few days after Christmas. It was about -40 F. This seemed a little cool after being in Calgary for Christmas where it was 0 to -10 F. It turned out the temperature was going to be a problem. Before the De Havilland Otter could take us to camp the temperature went down to -50 F and stayed below -40 F in the daytime, what there was of it. Apparently the pilot would not or could not fly when the temperature was below -40F. At the company's expense the crew stayed in the Inuvik hotel for about 4 days till the weather warmed up to -20 or -30 F.

I think you are imaging there may be mischief afoot with a number of teenagers full of piss and vinegar and little to do. Not to disappoint, there was. The party chief had a meeting with all of us warning about too much alcohol consumption and trouble with the authorities. His bottom line was no fraternizing with the natives. None of this seemed too onerous.

Days one and two were fairly uneventful. Walks around town, trips to the bar, reading a bunch of the books you brought to read in camp. On one of the walks around town we saw some thing we missed previously. It was a mountain of beer cases full of empty beer bottles. Probably 6 feet high, 4 feet wide and

20 feet long. We guessed they must be a waiting shipment south on a barge come summer. One evening there was an Inuit gentleman at the hotel with a polar bear hide for sale. It was not tanned but stretched out flat to dry to be sold to the Hudson Bay. I don't remember it being very large. He wanted $50 for it. It seemed like a good idea to buy it. That soon passed considering you had to keep it somewhere till you went home in the spring. Maybe if I could have folded it and put it in a box and shipped it home! It did not happen.

As time will do, it causes people to forget things they have been told. Bad judgment is usually there to fill the void. False bravado is coming up next. For those who do not drink but do observe, this is all very interesting, because you know if you continue to observe, the inevitable faux pas will take place. We did not have to wait long.

A younger member of the group whose memory had not developed to its full potential forgot the warning from the party chief. No fraternizing with the native ladies. Our observations unclouded by alcohol were in top form. Hence we noticed the amorous gazes exchanged across the bar between him and three young ladies of native descent.

It was not long and they were all sitting at the same table. The hither to glances had done their magic. Alcohol and time on your hands are trouble; it's a bad combination but the glances had done the rest.

Finally our patience was rewarded. He left the table with two of the young ladies. They headed for the stairs to the second floor. What else could you do but follow at a discreet distance to see what might happen? His roommate was in the bar so I guess he felt fairly safe taking the ladies to their shared room. As I remember it, his room was about halfway down the hall.

We arrived at the top of the stairs just in time to hear his door close.

Now it was time for some "thin'in'" (circa 1970 Yogi Bear) to go on. There is no way you can let an atrocity like this take place that might sully the reputation of all concerned. What to do?!

We went to a room just down the hall from the upcoming action to cogitate. All sorts of approaches were considered: banging on the door, making loud noise in the hallway, having someone else go to the room on some pretext. Any thing to upset the mood.

"Look at the transom. Can we use it somehow?" said one of the guys, looking over the door in the room we were in.

"We could throw cold water through it," said another. This was met with great gales of laughter from the farm boys.

"Wait a minute," came from the last man. He had just reached over and picked up a camera.

"We should be able to use this somehow."

The camera was examined by all of us. It had film. It belonged to one of the guys in the room. There were two important considerations.

"We need a camera with a flash. It will be too dark in there to get a picture without one. I know who has one," said one of the farm boys. "I'll go ask him to loan me his camera. I won't tell him what it's for."

"Go! Go! We don't know how long this will go on," we chorused.

He was gone. Down a few rooms was the man with the camera. While he was gone we tried to figure out how we could get up to the transom with the hotel furniture at hand.

The doors are 6'6", the transom about 16 inches wide and

the width of the door just above it. It opens in from the top being hinged above the door with a 6-inch chain at the top. We needed about 7'6" to get high enough to take a picture through the V-shaped opening the transom made when open, where there was no glass to deflect the flash.

Ability for the photographer to point the camera down was imperative. We felt the bed would be the action center. Room layout in the hotel was standard; whoever was going to take the picture would know where to point if there was no give-away noise.

We still had a problem: getting enough height to pull this off. Just as the man with the camera returned we had a brilliant idea. Instead of one of us going down to the room and standing on a suitcase trying to get high enough to get the job done, we would use a chair. Trying this in the room we occupied it seemed like a good idea. One of the guys got on the chair with the camera but could not get high enough to point the camera down affording the best exposure!

"There is only one thing left to do. Let's hold the chair, one of us on each side. The photographer will stand on top of the back of the chair. That should give lots of height," I said.

We tried it in the room we were in a couple of times. It worked fine. There were a couple of critical things that had to happen. Silence was paramount; any hint of activity outside his door would end it all. Aligning the straight-backed flat-topped chair, holding it so it did not tip against the door when the photographer climbed up, was critical. The photographer not banging himself or the camera on the door during his ascent up the chairs back to the transom was critical. We decided that two pictures would be our goal. The first one would be a surprise to everyone in the room. While they were figuring out what happened the second pic would be taken.

After that the photographer would jump off the chairback, run down the hall to the room we had just left with the door open. He would throw the camera on the bed and be ready to close the door very quickly and quietly when the chair bearers were back in the room. We made a couple more practice runs.

We opened the door checked the hall, no one in sight. We were off, the photographer behind the chair bearers, camera at the ready. We only had to go down two doors and across the hall. Bare feet are best for silence and no slipping while climbing chair backs and perching on their tops taking pics. He was there; we were looking up. There was a flash; a yell came from the room; another flash; the cameraman jumped and was gone, the rest of us running with the chair down the hall. We got into the room, everything went dark and you could barely hear the door closing.

"I know you guys did that! I'll get you for this!" he yelled.

He stomped past our door using language that defies description. Banging on a door two doors down, he yelled the name of one of the guys in our room. After receiving no response he went downstairs. Almost immediately the two ladies scurried down the hall and out the exit.

He accused crewmembers of perpetrating the picture prank, but he never got it quite right. You may think this is the end of the story. Wrong.

As you recall we had a grocery and mail plane that showed up weekly. The mail plane was very good at taking out exposed film and bringing back developed pictures, even slides. For lack of anything better to do, when anyone had developed slides returned we had a show. You know the pictures in question plus others. The camera owner requested and received six duplicates of slide numbers whatever. Prior to the show some of the slides in question were distributed to all those who were showing slides that night. Now how would you know who took the pictures?!

Show time. We were all crowded into the rec trailer, the screen up, the projector on, slides being shown. Almost everybody but him knew what's coming. Halfway through the first show there appeared a picture of a hotel room's interior taken from above. The figures in the picture were askew as the picture was taken at a peculiar angle. The room was dead silent — we're talking morgue quiet.

"You @%*^$#@! I knew somebody here did that; now I know."

A rear assault on the projectionist with intent to maim was at hand. Anticipated beforehand, he never made it. He got one step from his chair and was subdued. With him calmed down the show proceeded. The duplicate slides showed up periodically, eliciting a decreased reaction as the slides numbers increased. There was no way to know who the original perpetrators were and there still isn't.

As a footnote, I know you weren't reading this to find out how the wannabe Casanova made out. I will say this: the pictures revealed no inappropriate behavior, unless you count hands outside clothing.

EPILOGUE

If you have been following what has turned into a series of books about a Game Warden's life, you will *have* read *POACHERS CRANBERRIES & SNOWSHOES, POACHERS BEANS & BIRCH BARK; POACHER CHASER HOLIDAYS*; and now, our latest book, *ARCTIC to ALPINE* ; which in some ways, is a continuation of the previous books. It has one-of-a-kind stories about working and playing from Inuvik to New Orleans and in between that can only be imagined.

By the quantity of our previous books sold, it appears we've developed an increasing number of loyal readers who enjoy these strange but true stories.

I've had the good fortune to have an adventure-packed life; even so, there are only so many stories to be told.

There will be another book — about what and when will be determined on another day.

ENJOY

For additional copies of *ARCTIC to ALPINE, POACHERS CRANBERRIES & SNOWSHOES, POACHERS BEANS& BIRCH BARK* or *POACHER CHASER HOLIDAYS*, please contact the publisher JBS PUBLISHING, your local book store or our website.

To arrange author talks book signings or interviews you may contact the publisher

You may read stories out of each book on the web site.

JBS PUBLISHING
Rocky Mountain House,
AB T4T 2A3
email address: on Website
Website: jbspublishing.com
Phone: 1 403 845 4234